Green **Line**

Oberstufe Klasse 10

von
Niamh Humphreys
Ceri Marriott
Cheryl Pelteret
Anja Treinies

herausgegeben von
Harald Weisshaar

Ernst Klett Verlag
Stuttgart · Leipzig

Hallo liebe Schülerinnen und Schüler,

mit dem Vokabeltraining aktiv zu Green Line Oberstufe Klasse 10 kannst du die neuen Vokabeln aus deinem Englischbuch üben.

Es ist immer gut, neue Wörter in einem Satz zu lernen. Du findest daher zu jeder Seite in deinem Englischbuch unter „What do you remember?" englische Sätze oder kurze Texte, die du am besten mit Bleistift vervollständigen kannst. Solltest du einmal nicht weiter wissen, können dir die deutschen Übersetzungen der gefragen Vokabeln als Hilfestellung dienen. Deine Lösungen kannst du auf den Seiten 80–88 selbst überprüfen. Achte dabei auch auf die korrekte Schreibung der Wörter.

Zusätzlich gibt es noch viele Rätsel und andere spannende Aufgaben für dich, damit du die neuen Wörter üben und ausprobieren kannst. Diese findest du immer unten auf jeder Seite.

Viel Spaß und Erfolg mit deinem Vokabeltraining aktiv

Inhaltsverzeichnis

Topic 1 Growing up

→ pages 8–9

What do you remember?

(Ehe-)Mündigkeitsalter • Gericht • Rechte • Ehe • verpflichtend • Altersgrenzen • Zustimmung • Einerseits …, andererseits … • Zahlen

When you are growing up, a lot of changes happen in your life. ______________ you get more ______________ and you do not need your parents' ______________ for as many things any more, but ______________ you have new responsibilities, too. However this varies from country to country as you can see from the ______________ . ______________ show that the ______________ , for example, is 14 in Germany when your partner is under 18, but in the UK it is 16. In other countries, sex before ______________ is illegal; someone could be taken to ______________ if he or she breaks this law. School is ______________ in many countries, but there are also countries where a lot of children don't go to school at all.

1 Say it in a different way

Fill in the missing words. The two sentences must have the same meaning.

1. The court decided that he had to stay in prison for the rest of his life.
   → He was ______________________________ .
2. Children in Pakistan do not have to go to school.
   → School is not ______________________________ in Pakistan.
3. In Pakistan buying alcohol is not allowed.
   → In Pakistan buying alcohol is ______________________________ .

2 Reacting and commenting

In Germany drinking alcohol should be illegal for everyone.

It depends on … • On the one hand …, but on the other hand … • … should be protected • … could be dangerous • I never knew that … • I think/don't think it's appropriate … • I think it should be up to … to decide • I think the reason for this is … • I was surprised to see that … • Correct me if I'm wrong, but …

Give a short comment on the statement. Use three of the phrases in the box.

____

____

____

____

→ pages 10–14

What do you remember?

jmdn. zu etw. überreden • grob • Art • Also gut. • Narbe • ein paar Verbrechen begehen • berauben • schwören • Bedauern • widerstehen • vermeiden • fett

Barry was a ____________ and very ____________ 17-year-old guy with a huge ____________ on his face. He enjoyed any ____________ of dangerous situation and he had even ________________________, such as ____________ people. One day he ____________ his friend John ____________ helping him with his plan: to steal a car and drive around. At first John didn't want to help him because he always tried to ____________ doing things that were illegal, but Barry ____________ that he wouldn't have any ____________. In the end John couldn't ____________. "____________," he said before walking away.

3 Word search: Arguing and fighting

Find ten words in the puzzle that have to do with arguing and fighting. The words go →, ↓, ←, ↘ and ↙. Then write 3–5 sentences in which you use these words.

P	A	T	N	E	L	O	I	V	H	D
A	A	X	S	F	B	U	L	L	Y	B
I	D	G	K	T	E	B	Y	C	G	K
N	E	M	Y	A	R	V	L	D	U	W
J	C	E	T	Z	I	U	K	O	E	I
U	E	G	A	M	A	D	G	A	O	O
R	O	U	S	T	W	X	P	G	A	D
Y	I	L	C	Z	Z	O	K	O	L	E
U	O	N	A	F	N	H	J	P	L	E
I	O	M	R	E	C	K	L	E	S	S
Q	P	N	V	D	X	Z	I	E	M	L

____

____

____

____

____

____

____

→ pages 10–14

What do you remember?

sofort • Handschuhe • zurückweichen • verwundbar • einzeln – Knochen • ziehen • Mäntel • greifen • Angst • entdecken • unbeholfen • Brust • Wachdienst • überfluten

The next night Barry and John put on their ______________ and ______________ , and when they ______________ a nice car, Barry ______________ tried to break into it. "Watch out for any policemen or ______________ guards!" he said to John. But John felt ______________ and ______________ . He wasn't reckless like Barry. ______________ filled his ______________ and ______________ his whole body – every ______________ ______________ . He ______________ . When Barry saw this, he ______________ for John and ______________ him back to the car.

4 Words to do with crime and law

Put the words under the right heading. Sometimes there is more than one possible solution.

illegal • injury • theft • to break a law • to accuse sb of sth • to ban • age limit • legal • to attack sb • independence • privileges • to murder sb • assault • to commit a crime • rights • act • compulsory • self-defense • to rob sb

law	crime

5 Word formation

Change the words given to the form in brackets.

1. security → (verb) ______________
2. weight → (verb) ______________
3. to use → (noun) ______________
4. to marry → (noun) ______________
5. connection → (verb) ______________
6. to sort → (noun) ______________
7. responsibility → (adjective) ______________
8. thief → (noun) ______________
9. reference → (verb) ______________
10. to comprehend → (noun) ______________

→ pages 10–14

What do you remember?

Container • jmdn. einer Sache beschuldigen – Diebstahl • ausflippen • kämpfen • berühren • die Konsequenzen tragen • stolpern • kaum – kriechen • mithalten • Leiter • taumeln • zusammenrollen

John was starting to ______________ . "Don't ______________ me!" he said, "I don't want to ______________ ______________ . I'm sure we'll have to ______________ for this if we don't run now." The two boys started to ______________ . Suddenly two policemen came up to them. They had been watching the two boys from behind a ______________ . Barry and John started to run, but Barry was slow and could not ______________ with John. He ______________ over a ______________ that was lying on the floor and ______________ . John had easily jumped over the ladder before him. Barry was in so much pain that he could ______________ ______________ . He ______________ himself ______________ in a field nearby until the policemen were gone.

6 Odd word out

Which word does not fit? Cross it out and explain why.

1. glove • scar • coat • hat

   ______________ does not fit because ______________

2. compulsory • to ban • legal • bone

   ____

3. to spot • to drag • to notice • to see

   ____

4. to trip • to tumble • to stumble • to skip

   ____

5. to run • to freeze • to crawl • to walk

   ____

7 Opposites

Find the opposites of the following words.

1. thin • ______________
2. divorce • ______________
3. a long time • ______________
4. disagreement • ______________
5. illegal • ______________
6. many • ______________
7. gentle • ______________
8. behind • ______________

→ pages 10–14

What do you remember?

Verständnis • Umschlag • seinen Standpunkt deutlich machen • fließen • leugnen • nicht Schuld haben an • explodieren • stopfen • sicher befestigen – für den Fall, dass …

Don't ______________ your rubbish into that container! It is already full!

The letter came in a blue ______________ .

The bomb ______________ in the early afternoon, but fortunately nobody was killed.

I've made a lot of mistakes, but I'm not to ______________ everything.

In court he ______________ having committed the crime.

______________ the tent ______________ there is a storm tonight!

Well, you've ______________ . Now I believe you.

It has been raining all night. Now water is ______________ down the streets.

It helps the reader's ______________ of the story if you describe your characters' feelings.

8 Spot the mistakes

Find one mistake in each sentence and correct them.

1. He sworn that he was not to blame for the injury.
2. When I was young, I once made a crime.
3. Weight the advantages and disadvantages of the job before you apply for it.
4. You have to carry the consequences of the crime you have committed.

9 Words and their definitions

a) *Match the verbs with the right definitions.*

1. to linger	a) to fall quickly and without control
2. to tumble	b) to hit your foot against something or put your foot down awkwardly while you are walking
3. to skip	c) to take a long time to leave or disappear
4. to stumble	d) to move lightly and quickly, making a small jump after each step

b) *Find the words or phrases that are described by the following definitions.*

1. during the time that something else is happening: ______________
2. in spite of the fact that: ______________
3. a short period of time: ______________
4. all the time that something is happening: ______________

→ pages 10–14

What do you remember?

Leistung • Getreide • verbinden • hinauslehnen • Layout • Gebrauch – Selbstverteidigung • Unkraut

In the USA the ______________ of guns is allowed for ______________ .

Something is wrong! My computer won't ______________ to the Internet.

The farmer has huge fields of ______________ .

When you have a garden, ______________ can be really annoying.

It's dangerous to ______________ of a car window.

I like the ______________ of the poster.

Writing this book was the greatest ______________ of my life.

10 Synonyms

Replace the marked words with words which have the same or a very similar meaning.

1. She wanted to do some **kind** (→ ______________) of trick on her skateboard.
2. Water had **poured into** (→ ______________) every corner of the house.
3. He was full of **fear** (→ ______________).
4. Please **choose** (→ ______________) one of the CDs.
5. It was so dark that I could **hardly** (→ ______________) see and so I **tripped** (→ ______________) over a pile of garbage.
6. Many people have to fight (→ ______________) for their freedom.
7. When they ran away from the police, he **almost** (→ ______________) lost his way.

11 Bits and pieces

Match the syllables from the boxes and form words with four syllables.

se- • com- • ac- • com-

-com- • -pul- • -pre- • -cu-

-hen- • -ri- • -plish- • -so-

-ry • -ty • -ment • -sion

1. ______________
2. ______________
3. ______________
4. ______________

12 Find the missing word

1. two – one • double – ______________
2. tongue – mouth • heart – ______________
3. foot – shoe • hand – ______________
4. fear – dread • to pull – ______________

→ page 15

What do you remember?

gesamt, ganz • missverstanden • zu jmdm. aufschauen • Rand • mit Problemen belastet • vernachlässigt

Sally is a very ______________ teenager. She feels that she has spent her ______________ life living on the ______________ of society. She feels ______________ by her parents and ______________ by her teachers. When she meets Jeff, a cool skater, she thinks that she has found someone that she can ______________ …

13 A crossword

Across	Down
3. when you are easy to hurt or attack	1. a piece of clothing which you wear to keep your hands warm
5. the front part of your body between your neck and your stomach	2. to make something safe from being attacked
7. to stop yourself from doing something that you want to do	4. not relaxed or comfortable
10. a synonym for 'hardly'	6. having problems or difficulties
	8. a synonym for 'at once'
	9. a strong fear of something

→ pages 18–19

What do you remember?

kompliziert • obwohl • ein Kondom überziehen • sich der Wahrheit stellen • reif • fürchten • Humor • aufschieben • Reife • Spannung

Nick Hornby's *Slam* is a story full of black ________ and ________.

It is about 16-year-old Sam and his ________ path to ________.

On his sixteenth birthday he gets a text message from his former girlfriend Alicia, who thinks she might be pregnant. This is possible because there was one time when he hadn't ________ anything ________. Sam ________ finding out the result of the pregnancy test, but he cannot ________ it ________ forever. He has to ________, ________ he would rather deny it and spend all of his time on his skateboard. Later, Sam becomes more ________ and takes responsibility for his son Roof.

14 How does the text say it?

Fill in the words that are used in the excerpt of Slam *in your textbook without looking at the text again.*

1. It looked like I had to do it, although I would rather do anything else.

   → I didn't see how I could do anything else, ________ I wanted to do anything else. (l. 24f)

2. […] because she knew that we'd been out the evening before.

   → […] because she knew we'd been out the ________ evening. (l. 9)

3. I hoped that their orders would take a lot of time to make.

   → I hoped they had the longest and most ________ orders Starbucks had ever heard of. (l. 55f)

4. I love you too, my dear.

   → I love you too, ________. (l. 34)

15 Mixed bag: First date

Complete the words.

Megan met her s________ Brian at Starbucks. She was having a cappuccino and a d________ when suddenly a note was thrown onto her table. She was so surprised that she n________ s________ her cappuccino. Someone had s________ a question on the note which said: "S________ I asked you out for a drink, what would you do?" When she looked up, she saw Brian and liked him s________ a________. "I'd say, it's a d________," she wrote back.

→ pages 18–19

What do you remember?

Saft • Donuts • sofort • häufiger Partnerwechsel • Abmachung • kritzeln • andauern • verrückt werden • außer • Lappen • aufwischen • verschütten • zweifellos • Angenommen …

Homer Simpson loves ______________ .

If you don't find a job ______________ , you shouldn't give up trying.

I know you are in a difficult situation, but it won't ______________ forever.

My little sister ______________ her glass of orange ______________ when we were in the café, and I had to ______________ it ______________ with a ______________ . If she does it again, I'll ______________ , ______________ .

Don't ______________ on this piece of paper. It has got important information on it.

I don't eat any meat, ______________ chicken.

Let's make a ______________ : I'll help you with French and you help me with Maths.

______________ is one of the reasons for the spread of sexually transmitted diseases.

______________ you won a million dollars, what would you buy?

16 Problem page

Here is a message that a 16-year-old girl sent to a problem page on the Internet. Write a short answer to her. Use at least three of the following words or phrases.

to dread sth • to face the truth • complicated • to put sth off • mature • to go mad • immature • even though

Please help!
Hi there! I hope that you can help me because I'm really in trouble. Two weeks ago I had sex with my boyfriend. Of course he'd put something on, but it broke … Now I'm late … I dread the result of the pregnancy test … What can I do now? (Girl, 16 years)

____

____

____

____

____

____

____

→ pages 20–23

What do you remember?

Rede • Jahrestag • bestimmt, sicherlich • Nominierungen • Benzin • (hier:) tendieren zu • Schluss machen • dankbar sein • uneingeladen zu einer Party kommen • sich für etw. entscheiden • ehrlich gesagt • Rückmeldung • Gewohnheiten • stören

Jenny's boyfriend ______ with her just after their third ______ .

______ , I can understand him. She had so many strange ______ that ______ him. You know, she ______ every ______ .

Let's stop at the gas station. We need some ______ .

What are your ______ for the class president? Please write them down.

The people's ______ to the president's ______ was very negative, because he only described the problems of the country. He should have given the solutions as well.

– I'm very ______ by these expensive shoes.

– If I were you, I would ______ the cheaper ones over there.

They are ______ not happy with all the changes he wants to make.

I'd ______ if you could have a look at my essay.

17 Prepositions

Fill in the missing prepositions.

1. The age ______ consent is 16 in the UK.
2. On holiday Becky ran ______ a friend she had not seen for five years.
3. Last year Ben was accused ______ theft.
4. I tried to keep ______ with the man, but he was too fast.
5. Don't blame me ______ your problems!
6. Do you know why Pete broke ______ with his girlfriend?

18 Synonyms

Find synonyms for the following words.

1. number • ______
2. a short time • ______
3. almost • ______
4. whole • ______
5. to split up • ______
6. although • ______
7. apart from • ______
8. to choose • ______
9. a few • ______
10. reply • ______

→ pages 24–25

What do you remember?

zusammenbrechen • Einstellung • Priorität • dämlich • jmdm. ein Vorbild sein • naiv • bestätigen • Frühstückspension • wohingegen • Prioritäten setzen • gültig • die Stirn runzeln

Stop talking like this! You're not ______________________ to your little brother.

When she heard the bad news, she ______________________ and cried.

I don't like your ______________________ school. You must ______________________ the right ______________________ for yourself.

Playing in a rock band is my highest ______________________ .

I'm sorry, the manager has ______________________ that your ticket is not ______________________ .

My friend ______________________ at me. He thinks I'm really ______________________ , ______________________ I believe I'm just a little ______________________ sometimes.

When we go to London, we could sleep at a ______________________ .

19 Say it in a different way

Use the words and phrases on the right to say the sentences in a different way.

1. What happened last summer is not my mistake! **to be to blame for sth**

   → ______________________

2. Last night a 50-year-old man was killed with a knife. **to murder**

   → ______________________

3. The police reported that 31 paintings were stolen. **theft**

   → ______________________

4. I think drinking alcohol should not be allowed for young people under 18. **to ban**

   → ______________________

5. If you do something illegal, you have to face the consequences. **to commit a crime**

   → ______________________

6. After having been arrested, the thief was taken to the police station at once. **straight away**

   → ______________________

   ____

7. The victim of the assault had to be taken to hospital because she was seriously hurt. **injury**

   → ______________________

   ____

20 Words and their definitions: Crime and law

a) *Match the words from the box with the right definitions.*

age limit • compulsory • self-defense • theft • independence • illegal • right • assault • legal • injury

1.		the state of being free to decide and do what you want to do
2.		not being allowed by the law
3.		the age at which a person is allowed or not allowed to do something
4.		a violent attack
5.		when you have to do something because of a rule or law
6.		damage to your body caused by an accident or an attack
7.		the act of stealing
8.		something that you are allowed to do or have
9.		something you do to protect yourself or your property
10.		being allowed by law

b) *Write down three more words from the lexical field together with their definitions.*

____

____

____

21 Characters

How would a character behave if he/she could be described by the following adjectives? Give examples.

1. **naive:**

____

____

2. **mature:**

____

____

3. **responsible:**

____

____

4. **immature:**

____

____

5. **troubled:**

____

____

Topic 2 Multi-ethnic Britain

→ pages 28–29

What do you remember?

afrokaribisch • ethnisch • Bande, Gang • weder noch • schwarzafrikanisch • Bürger • Prozentsatz • Mehrheit • bangladeschisch

Some areas of London have become attractive to tourists because of the high __________ of people from different __________ backgrounds. For example, people go to Brick Lane – or 'Banglatown' – to eat at restaurants run by __________ immigrants. Tourists looking for __________ or __________ culture love the Notting Hill festival. However, the idea that Notting Hill is an affordable, multi-cultural part of London, is no longer based on reality. Once known for __________ problems and crime, it is now home to high-income __________.
And even in a London full of people who have Asian or African backgrounds, the __________ of people with a high income have __________. Rich people are still usually white.

1 A crossword

Across

4. a person who lives in a country and has all the rights of its people
7. a person from Pakistan
8. a group of people who stick together and are sometimes violent or criminal

Down

1. facts or statistics
2. the way that we see or understand something
3. more than half of a group
5. a group of countries ruled by an emperor, king or queen
6. a kind of large farm where coffee, sugar etc. is grown

→ pages 28–29

What do you remember?

Daten • Plantagen • Pakistaner • Sklavenhandel • Reich • abstammen von • Massen-

__________ immigration to the UK started in the late 1940s. The __________ show that 1948 was the first year when large numbers of men started arriving from the Caribbean. They were mostly 'Afro-Caribbean' – people __________ the Africans who had been brought to the Caribbean as part of the __________. Their grandparents had worked on the __________ during the days of the British __________. These were not the only immigrants, of course. During the 1950s and 1960s, for example, large numbers of __________, Indians and Bangladeshis arrived. Today people of South Asian origin are the largest non-white ethnic group in Britain.

2 Word pairs

Match the words and complete the sentences with the word pairs.

ethnic • trade • immigration • minority • mass • slave

1. Sometimes life can be more difficult when you are part of an __________.
2. In the days of the British Empire, some people became rich through the __________.
3. In Britain __________ started after the Second World War.

3 Discussing statistics

Write comments on the pie chart using three of the following phrases.

The pie chart shows that … • The statistics / numbers show that … • The majority / minority of … • Less / more than half … • …% of the pupils … • I'm (not) surprised (to see / to learn) that … • I can / can't understand why … • I think the results of the survey … • I think the results of a survey in … would be …

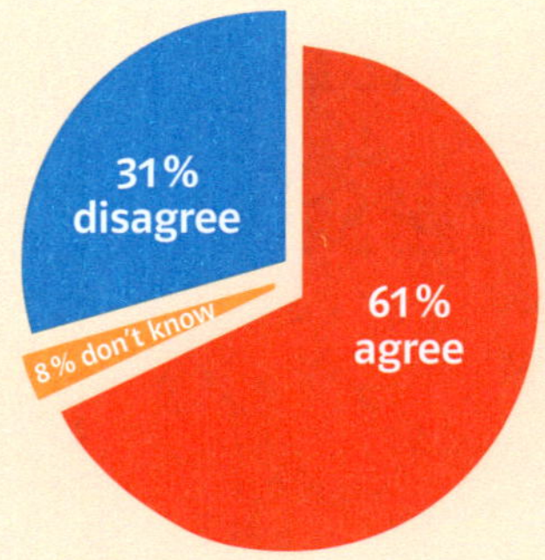

"I would like our school to be more multi-cultural." – Do you agree or disagree?

→ pages 30–31

What do you remember?

Fehlschlag • afrokaribisch • Lohn • betreiben • mieten • obwohl • Bedingungen • niemand sonst • jede Menge • Leidenschaft • sich richten an • jmdn. zu etw. antreiben • Durchschnitts- • beitragen

My favourite place to eat is an ______________ restaurant in Brixton. My cousin ______________ it. He has a real ______________ for cooking and offers ______________ delicious African and Caribbean dishes. In the beginning, his family was afraid his restaurant would be a ______________ . He ______________ a space that ______________ wanted in an unpopular part of town. However his cooking was not ______________ the rich and famous and he didn't expect to be listed in ______________ restaurant guides. He just wanted to ______________ something nice to the neighbourhood, and he has. People like working for him, ______________ he can't pay a high ______________ . Other working ______________ are good and the restaurant has a great atmosphere. I ______________ you to try it!

4 Word formation

Form the nouns from these verbs. Sometimes the word form does not change.

1. to fail • ______________
2. to rent • ______________
3. to serve • ______________
4. to abuse • ______________
5. to secure • ______________
6. to encounter • ______________
7. to present • ______________
8. to treat • ______________
9. to recognize • ______________
10. to use • ______________

5 Mixed bag: A travel agent

Complete the text with nouns from exercise 4.

I run a travel agency for people who want to travel to the Caribbean. The ______________ for my office is high but a good office is important. I'm optimistic: I offer a very good ______________ and I don't believe my business will be a ______________ . I've never suffered racial ______________ at work. I once had a frightening ______________ with a man who wanted to rob the office, but that was very unusual and there is no need for extra ______________ . I love my work!

→ pages 30–31

What do you remember?

Mieten • Vorurteile • auf etw. drängen • Aufgaben • Wohlstand • vergangene, -r, -s • Nachkriegs- • harte Behandlung • Heimweh haben • Missbrauch • Begegnungen • ablehnen

Many of the ________ immigrants to Britain suffered ________ at work, paid high ________ and had to deal with negative opinions and ________ in everyday life. Some even suffered physical ________ and were very ________ . They had wanted a part of Britain's ________ and now felt the present was as bad as the ________ years. However, my Jamaican grandfather said his first ________ with English people were positive. At work, he ________ doing boring ________ and his colleagues ________ a better position for him, where he could contribute his skills. He was soon successful and happy.

6 Prepositions

Fill in the missing prepositions.

1. I don't object ________ working hard when it helps my business.
2. My family is descended ________ African slaves.
3. You can find a host ________ African products at markets in Brixton.
4. Our products are aimed ________ international customers.
5. We are pressing ________ equality in the workplace.
6. The market is divided ________ different sections.
7. The majority ________ immigrants want to stay in Britain.

7 Mixed bag: Grandmother

Complete the words.

My grandmother is from Trinidad. She misses the sunshine, and when she thinks of p ________ times, she sometimes gets h ________ . She has a p ________ for Caribbean food and the c ________ of her kitchen cupboards is amazing – every possible kind of spice! I think she should l ________ a catering business but she says she's too old. It's a pity because n ________ o ________ e ________ can cook like her! But at least she can c ________ to keeping up memories of her home country.

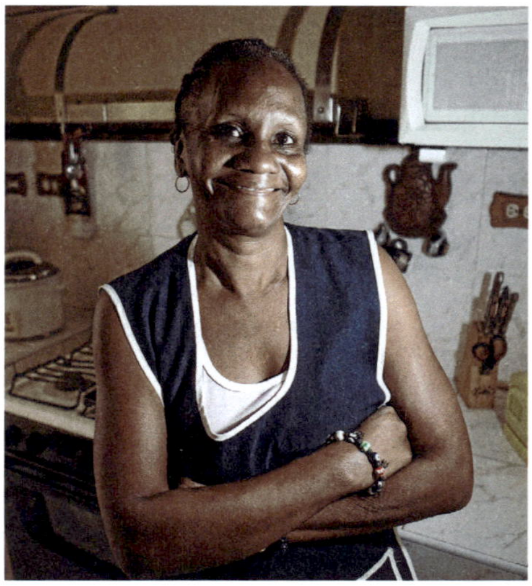

→ pages 30–31

What do you remember?

überall in • Start • Komplexität • Dienstleistung • karibisch • Inhalt • Einrichtungen • unterteilen • Bereiche • einschließen • Herkunft

Sometimes immigrants who have lived in Britain for a long time want to find a home in the country of their ______________ when they get older. My grandparents did that and so I learnt about the ______________ of a move to another country. I'm now starting a business to help other people to do it. I'm ______________ my ______________ into two ______________ : the 'homes' part will find homes ______________ the whole ______________ area and the 'moving' service will ______________ help in dealing with ______________ like banks. We're having a big party for the ______________ of the company next week and we're producing a brochure. Its ______________ is exciting: beautiful homes in Jamaica and Trinidad!

8 Say it in a different way

Use the words and phrases on the right to say the sentences in a different way.

1. Max wants to do something for the prosperity of his town. **to contribute**

   ____

2. You can find Indian restaurants all over the city. **throughout**

   ____

3. Do you understand how complex the situation is? **complexity**

   ____

4. Things were not always easy for the generation that lived after the war. **post-war**

   ____

5. The building I live in is old and dirty. **bad condition**

   ____

6. My boss always gives me the most boring things to do. **tasks**

   ____

9 Synonyms

Replace the marked words with words which have the same or a very similar meaning.

1. He wanted to contribute to the **wealth** (→ ______________) of his society.
2. She got a job but her **pay** (→ ______________) was low.
3. Martin works as a **hairdresser for men** (→ ______________).
4. Kath **manages** (→ ______________) her own business.

→ page 37

What do you remember?

zuständig • gelegentlich • Opfer • basieren auf • Komiker

Humour can help solve problems and the work of a ______________________ can be very important. The ______________________ joke can make your day better and if you can laugh about being the ______________________ of prejudice, it can help you feel stronger. Comedy that is ______________________ real problems is often the best, and it makes people think. I know someone who is ______________________ of comedy shows at a TV channel and he says comedy is the most serious thing in the world!

10 A puzzle

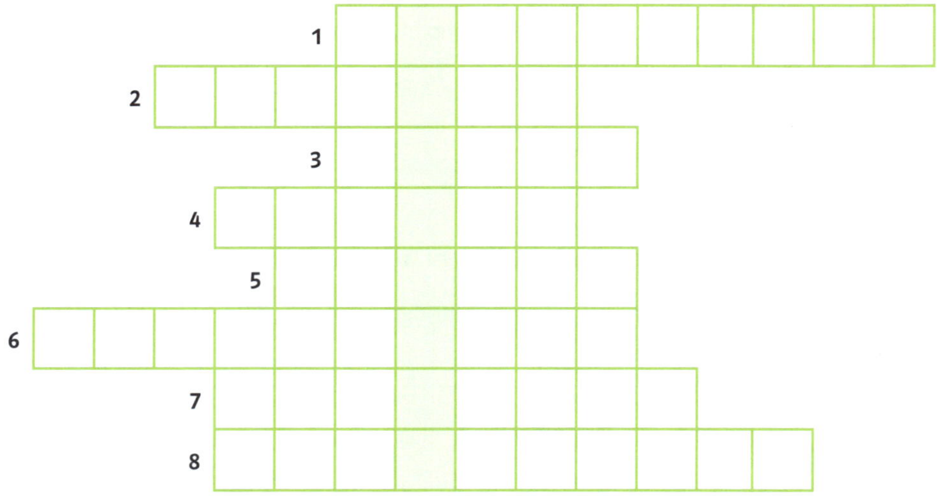

1. not regular, happening from time to time
2. the opposite of success
3. a person who is 'owned' by another, and who has to work for no money
4. a person who has been robbed, hurt or killed by another person
5. the start of a new business or product
6. popular with most people
7. a person whose job it is to make others laugh
8. another word for 'wealth'

Solution: ____

11 Mixed bag: Asian-British

Complete the text with words from exercise 10.

After the Second World War Asians played a role in the growing ______________________ of Britain and you can still see the effects today. Curry mixes which were once exotic are now ______________________ products in British shops. Unfortunately, there is also ______________________ violence against people with Asian backgrounds but almost everybody finds this shocking and wrong. The attempts of some criminals to make Asians want to leave Britain have always ended in ______________________ .

→ pages 40–41

What do you remember?

Beweis • verpflichtend • Dolmetscher • ermutigen • verwirrt • gewinnen • entschlossen • jmdn. davon abhalten, etw. zu tun • (*hier:*) Agentur, Büro • Einwohner

I speak two languages and I don't get ____________ . It's easy. Speaking Urdu with my family doesn't ____________ me ____________ being integrated in British society. Some foreign parents are ____________ to give their children the best start, so they speak English at home. However, there is no ____________ that you speak English better if you only speak English. I ____________ a lot by speaking two languages: I work as an ____________ for a language and translation ____________ . Many ____________ of my town need our help but they are learning English, too. I'm not sure if English lessons should be ____________ but we should definitely ____________ everyone to learn English.

12 Say it in a different way

Fill in the missing words. The two sentences must have the same meaning.

1. My job is to repeat what people say in a different language.
   → I work as an ____________ .
2. I love this city because there are so many different people here.
   → I love this city for its ____________ .
3. £2.5 billion is a lot of money.
   → £2.5 billion is a very high ____________ .
4. If you're not happy about this, you should tell people.
   → If you're not happy about this, you should ____________ .
5. They thought she was not intelligent because she couldn't speak their language.
   → They ____________ her unintelligent because she couldn't speak their language.
6. Don't drink too much alcohol. It's unhealthy and dangerous!
   → Don't ____________ drinking alcohol. It's unhealthy and dangerous!

13 Words and their definitions

Complete the definitions of the following words.

1. **mosque:** a place where ____________
2. **residents:** the people who ____________
3. **comedian:** a person whose ____________
4. **presenter:** a person who ____________

→ pages 42–45

What do you remember?

drucken • Hammer • Umzüge • entschiedene Ansichten über etw. haben • Ruhe

There are ______________ to celebrate all kinds of things in Britain, for example the end of a war or a historical event. These kinds of celebrations can help you learn about your own culture and give you a sense of who you are. However, a group of young people who ______________ immigration recently caused trouble at a Chinese parade in my neighbourhood. They ______________ negative stories about Asian immigrants. Then, one Chinese boy was hit with a ______________ . He was really lucky that people who saw the attack helped him. He's OK now. He just needs ______________ .

14 Jumbled words

Put the letters in the right order and complete the table.

editoni • rear • shoomrum • trinp • oockyre oobk • conseic • pede-fidre • ngaoric • mja • ugaesas

Books, magazines and texts	Food and cooking

15 Word class

Say whether the words in exercise 14 are adjectives, nouns or verbs.

1. **adjectives:** ______________
2. **nouns:** ______________
3. **verbs:** ______________

16 Opposites

Find the opposites of the following words.

1. well-done • ______________
2. not to care about sth • ______________
3. tasteless • ______________
4. success • ______________
5. majority • ______________
6. to lose • ______________

→ pages 42–45

What do you remember?

pikant • Verkaufsstände • Küche • Kochbücher • Roastbeef • Yorkshirepudding • Orangensaft • Mineral- • gut durch(gebraten) • Essig • Butter • gebackene Bohnen • Haferbrei • Tomate • blutig, nur leicht angebraten

Portobello Road is a good place to get food. At the ______________ on the Portobello Road market or in the restaurants you can buy food from all over the world. If you're thirsty, you can get fresh ______________ or a pot of tea at one of the many cafés. There's a bookshop in the road that only sells ______________ so you can learn how to make classic British dishes like ______________ with ______________. Or, if you want to cook something ______________, have a look at their great section on Indian ______________.

I am a vegetarian and for breakfast I normally make myself a bowl of ______________. A hot breakfast with a fried ______________ and some ______________ and toast and ______________ is great, too. For dinner I normally prefer healthy salads but I do like chips with salt and ______________, as well. I don't understand how anyone can eat a ______________ steak. All that blood! Even ______________ steak is horrible. I drink juice and ______________ water. Boring? No! I love feeling healthy!

17 Word pairs

Match the words and complete the sentences with the word pairs.

roast • book • cookery • pudding • Yorkshire • steak • baked • beef • orange • beans • well-done • juice

1. I'm thirsty. Have you got any ______________?
2. I love ______________, but when it's rare, I can't eat it.
3. My other favourite type of meat is ______________.
4. It sounds like a dessert but you actually eat ______________ with meat.
5. We can open a tin of ______________ and eat them on toast.
6. You don't need a ______________ to tell you how to open a tin.

18 Spot the mistakes

Find one mistake in each sentence and correct them.

1. I don't like noodles but I love reis.
2. He feels strong about racism.
3. The Young Service can help stop teenagers getting involved in crime.
4. Caribbean traditions are at the head of the Notting Hill Carnival.
5. Nothing is more delicious than Afro-Caribbean kitchen!

→ pages 42–45

What do you remember?

Hochzeit • Judaismus • Einzel- • Tempel • Islam • Faktor • Hindu • Buddhismus • Christentum • Identität

__________ people with an Indian background, for example, love to have a big __________. Buddhists sometimes have smaller weddings because in __________, whether or not you get married is an __________ decision and not part of your religious __________. The style of Muslim weddings often has more to do with the culture of the man and woman than with __________ itself. In __________, the classic image of a wedding is of a bride in a white dress. At Jewish weddings the number seven is sometimes a __________ because it is a special number in __________. These weddings can be held at any location: it doesn't have to be a synagogue or __________.

19 Odd word out

Which word does not fit? Cross it out and explain why.

1. Christianity • Islam • Hindu • Judaism

   __________ does not fit because __________

2. rare • sensitive • well-done • spicy

   ____

3. butter • tomatoes • salad • green beans

   ____

4. follower • Buddhist • factor • interpreter

   ____

5. to print • well-done • edition • cookery book

   ____

20 Mixed bag: Who eats what?

Complete the words.

A full English breakfast is not the best way for a Muslim to start the day because it includes s __________ and bacon. In I __________, eating pork is not allowed. If you have a visitor from India, you should be careful about offering them r __________ b __________. If they are a H __________, they may not want to eat meat from a cow. British Christians eat most types of food. C __________ has few rules about what people may eat. British food is not very s __________ but most people love going to Indian restaurants for a really good curry.

21 Words and their definitions: Ethnic diversity and the fight for equality

a) *Match the words from the box with the right definitions.*

integration • nationality • ancestor • extremist • immigrant • to tolerate • racist • to campaign for • discrimination • racial equality

1.		a person who has left his or her own country to live somewhere else
2.		treating a person or a particular group of people in an unfair way
3.		a situation in which people of all races are treated in the same way
4.		when people become part of a society and are accepted by others
5.		a person who believes that people of their own race are better than others
6.		to organize a number of activities to try to achieve something
7.		to accept behaviour and beliefs which are different from your own
8.		a member of your family who lived a long time ago
9.		the official right to belong to a particular country
10.		a person who has very extreme ideas

b) *Write down three more words from the lexical field together with their definitions.*

___

___

___

22 An interview

A journalist interviews Tariq, the grandson of Pakistani immigrants. Write down Tariq's answers.

Journalist: When did your grandparents come to Britain?
Tariq: (*Tariq sagt, dass sie als Teil der Masseneinwanderung in den Nachkriegsjahren nach Großbritannien gekommen sind.*)

___

___

Journalist: What was hard for them about living here?
Tariq: (*Tariq sagt, dass sie Rassendiskriminierung erfahren haben.*)

___

Journalist: Was life easier for your parents?
Tariq: (*Tariq sagt, dass das Leben für seine Eltern einfacher gewesen ist. Sie haben manchmal Vorurteile erfahren, aber auch Anerkennung für ihre harte Arbeit.*)

___

___

Journalist: Are you British, or Pakistani, or British-Pakistani?
Tariq: (*Tariq sagt, er ist Brite. Ihm gefällt seine pakistanische Herkunft, aber sie hält ihn nicht davon ab, 100 % britisch zu sein. Er findet, das ist das Tolle an einer Vielvölkergesellschaft.*)

___

___

Topic 3 The Blue Planet

→ pages 48–49

What do you remember?

erneuerbar • Schaden – Verschmutzung • erzeugen – alternative, -r, -s • erneuerbar • globale Erwärmung • Bewusstsein schärfen, sensibilisieren • Klimawandel • ergänzen, erweitern

__________ and __________ are important environmental issues that have been discussed by scientists all over the world. They have led many politicians and non-governmental organisations to attempt to __________ of the __________ __________ is doing to our environment: and with some success. Many people care more about the environment today than they did in the past. In a number of countries governments have __________ the promotion of __________ energy sources to their list of priorities. Since our supplies of oil, gas, and coal will not last forever, it is important to __________ __________ forms of energy.

1 Word pairs

Make common expressions from a noun and an adjective. Use all the words in the box only once.

toxic • fresh • change • warming • group • air • plant • rain • power • gas • pressure • natural • acid • recycling • global • carbon • pure • climate • poisonous • solar • waste • dioxide • water • resources

1. __________ 4. __________ 7. __________ 10. __________

2. __________ 5. __________ 8. __________ 11. __________

3. __________ 6. __________ 9. __________ 12. __________

2 Word formation

Change the words given to the form in brackets.

1. to share → (noun) __________
2. protection → (verb) __________
3. to emit → (noun) __________
4. poison → (adjective) __________
5. to waste → (noun) __________
6. address → (verb) __________
7. to damage → (noun) __________
8. different → (verb) __________

3 Spot the mistakes

Find one mistake in each sentence and correct them.

1. Cars are more environmental friendly today than they were in the past.
2. At the meeting we should adress the company's biggest problems.
3. Organisations like WWF try to raise awareness for environmental issues.
4. Tomorrow there will be protests against the new offcoast windfarm.

→ pages 48–49

What do you remember?

Kohlendioxid – Emissionen, Ausstöße • aussterben • Drittel • Süßwasser • Zahlen • (sich) verdreifachen • Arten, Spezies • umweltfreundlich • rein

__________ recently published by the British government showed that a __________ of the country's __________ is less __________ than it was ten years ago. This figure is frightening. The warning that __________ __________ are predicted to __________ in the next ten years is also very worrying. Although our society has become more __________, more rare __________ are still likely to __________. Maps given with the figures were coloured in red, orange and green to illustrate which areas were most, and least at risk.

4 A Quiz

Answer the following questions without looking at your book.

1. About how many pounds of garbage are thrown away by each person every day?

   ____

2. How much of the earth's surface is covered by water?

   ____

3. How many species of plants and animals become extinct every day due to human influence?

   ____

4. By how much is the world's population expected to have grown by the year 2100?

   ____

5 Words about the environment

Are the words positive or negative for the environment? Write them under the correct heading.

damage • pollution • to campaign for • plastic • recycling plant • toxic • waste • renewable • emission • blackbird • to become extinct • solar • pressure group • windfarm • butterfly • pure • environmentally friendly • poisonous • carbon dioxide • to protect • farmers' market

Positive	Negative

→ pages 48–49

What do you remember?

Müll • Schmetterlinge • Plastik • Amseln • giftig – Gase • Bauernmärkte • ansprechen • Kanäle • Ausrede, Entschuldigung • giftig • Strophe • jmdm. zusagen, jmdm. gefallen

How to ______________ the serious issues caused by different types of ______________ pollution is a problem faced not only by governments, but also by our local communities. ______________ ______________ escaping into the atmosphere can have very bad effects on our natural surroundings. ______________ materials, such as ______________ bottles thrown into ______________ , may not only look horrible but can also seriously affect the wildlife which lives and feeds there. A recent survey of our local area has shown that ______________ and ______________ are declining in number; pollution has been identified as a significant factor for this fall. The local council has now asked all school children to write one ______________ poems on the subject, which will appear on large posters around the town. Local people should then have little ______________ for not knowing about the effects of pollution. Many town councils are promoting ______________ . Having such fresh local products available ______________ both town and country residents.

6 A puzzle

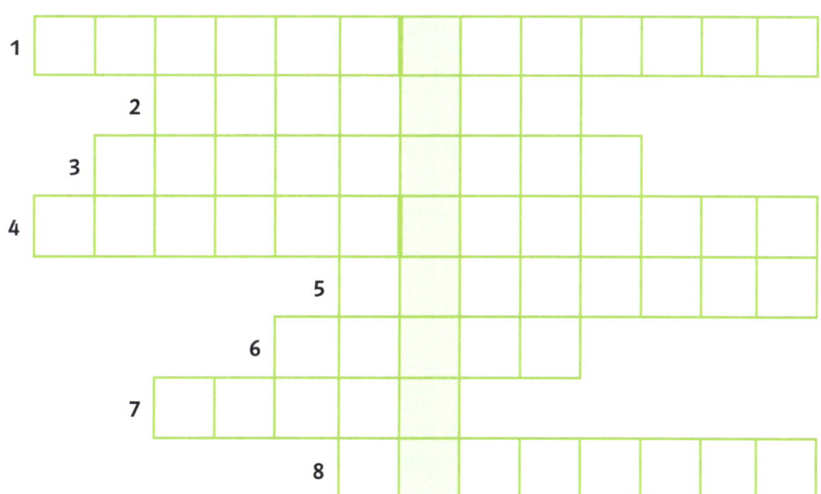

1. a gradual increase in the overall temperature of the earth's atmosphere
2. a group of animals or plants which can reproduce with each other
3. causing death or illness if taken into the body
4. a type of gas that can cause damage to the environment when there is too much of it in the atmosphere
5. in the sea but not far from the coast
6. the part of something that you own or are responsible for
7. relating to the sun
8. the act of sending out a gas or other substance into the air

Solution: ______________________________

→ pages 48–49

What do you remember?

vor der Küste gelegen – Windparks • Anteil • (*hier:*) Zukunft • verdienen • demonstrieren (für), aufmerksam machen (auf) • Wiederaufbereitungsanlage • (*hier:*) Industrie • international – Interessenverbände • (be)schützen

__________ __________ have been __________ against __________ __________ in order to raise awareness of environmental issues and to __________ the natural environment. __________ will see an organised protest outside the large __________ on the edge of town. The protesters will hand out leaflets which express the belief that future generations do not __________ to have to live on a planet polluted by today's population. The leaflet will encourage voters in the next election to think as seriously about the environment as the __________ so that everyone on the planet can have a fair __________ of the earth's resources.

7 Odd word out

Which word does not fit? Cross it out and explain why.

1. pollution • waste • resource • emission

   __________ does not fit because __________

2. nuclear power • people power • wind power • solar power

   ____

3. to produce • to generate • to make • to recycle

   ____

4. global warming • climate change • pressure group • acid rain

   ____

5. third • second • three • to triple

   ____

8 Words and their definitions: Verbs

Complete the verbs.

1. to produce heat, electricity, or another form of energy: to g __________
2. to lead or take part in a series of actions intended to achieve a particular result: to c __________
3. to keep someone or something safe from damage: to p __________
4. a synonym for 'to die out': to b __________
5. to have earned something by good or bad actions or behaviour: to d __________
6. when something is attractive and interesting for someone: to a __________

→ pages 50–51

What do you remember?

(auf)steigen • Meeres- • Verpackungen • Dokumentation • Giftstoffe • Seevögel • hawaiianisch • Hälse • Nahrungskette • ernst, hoffnungslos • (*hier:*) brauchen um sich abzubauen • Krise • Küken

A recent ______________ has shown how the environmental ______________ around the ______________ islands has been caused by huge amounts of plastic rubbish which are washed onto Hawaii's beaches every year. The situation for Hawaii's ______________ life, the beaches, ______________ and their ______________ is ______________ . The environmental dangers include hidden ______________ , which enter and ______________ the ______________ , and more obvious dangers, such as discarded ______________ which simply remains in the ocean and may become stuck in the ______________ of these creatures. The disastrous effects will ______________ a very long time because plastic is non-biodegradable.

9 Words and their definitions

Match the words on the left with the correct definition on the right.

1. to break down	a) a state of not knowing
2. to weep	b) very bad or serious
3. attitude	c) to be confronted with something
4. to list	d) to lose control and show emotion
5. ignorance	e) a person who buys and uses products and services
6. consumer	f) the opinions and feelings that you usually have about something
7. desperate	g) to write things down, one after another
8. to face	h) to cry, especially because you feel very sad

10 Synonyms

Replace the marked words with words which have the same or a very similar meaning.

1. The **reaction** (→ ______________) to the documentary was amazing. Everybody wanted to help.
2. The water which you drink is not totally **clean** (→ ______________) at all.
3. Please don't throw your **garbage** (→ ______________) into the forest.
4. Be careful! I don't know if these berries are **poisonous** (→ ______________).
5. Her face showed her **feelings** (→ ______________) when she saw her friends leaving.
6. Toxins enter and **move up** (→ ______________) the food chain which can be dangerous for humans as well.
7. We should talk very **quietly** (→ ______________). I don't want the others to hear us.
8. When she saw the dying seabirds, she started to **cry** (→ ______________).

→ pages 50–51

What do you remember?

Unwissenheit • sich einer Sache bewusst sein • Müll • aufräumen • Ausmaß • Bürsten • Einstellungen, Haltungen • umgeben von • Kette • Stecker, Stöpsel • Forscher • Tastaturen • Kämme • vorfinden • Gegenstände • Verpackungen • Lippenstifte • sterbend

The ______ of the environmental problem caused by ______ on the ______ of Hawaiian islands made ______ Charles Moore and camerawoman Rebecca Hosking desperate to change ______. They want to cure people's ______ and make them ______ their responsibility towards the environment, instead of ignoring it.

In an attempt to raise awareness of this crisis, the documentary by Rebecca Hosking and her team shows volunteers on Kamilo beach working to ______ and to rescue creatures suffering due to pollution caused by plastic waste. The volunteers are ______ ______ wildlife. They regularly ______ odd ______ such as old ______, ______, half-used ______, ______ of all sorts, ______, DVDs, and ______.

11 Plan a speech

Write a short speech in which you plan to give your audience five important environmental facts. Use the vocabulary in the box (and any other vocabulary you remember) to help you present your facts.

90% marine litter • plastic   plastic • 400–1000 years to degrade   300 million years • form oil
oil • make plastic   7/10 Earth = water   much more oxygen produced by oceans than by rainforests

______

______

______

______

______

______

______

12 Opposites

Find the opposites of the following words.

1. national • ______
2. question • ______
3. salt water • ______
4. to litter • ______
5. aware • ______
6. to scream • ______
7. to laugh • ______
8. to destroy • ______

→ pages 50–51

What do you remember?

sich einer Sache nicht bewusst sein • betreiben • Rückmeldung • kommen, erscheinen • Metzger/-in • Stückchen (von) • fungieren als • schütten • flüstern • Verbot • Presse • einfallen in • Handel, Gewerbe

Back home in Devon, Rebecca Hosking invited local traders to view her documentary. The ______________ to the invitation was extremely good; most of the town's traders ______________ to the film showing. They were completely ______________ the environmental problems associated with plastic. "I had no idea ______________ of plastic ______________ sponges for the chemicals we ______________ into the sea," said one trader. To make the most of this response to her documentary, Rebecca's friend, the local ______________, ______________ to her that she should propose a ______________ on the use of plastic bags in the local shops. The traders all voted for the ban. Hearing of this ______________ from around the world ______________ on the town of Modbury. As a result many towns and cities ______________ campaigns following Modbury's example and banned the use of non-biodegradable bags, without ______________ suffering.

13 Word search: Animals

Find nine animals in the puzzle and translate the words into German. The words go →, ↓, ↑, ←, ↘ and ↗.

Y	Y	S	D	E	X	T	L	A	S	W	H	B	X	T	W
L	D	E	K	O	S	F	B	U	E	L	A	H	W	X	O
F	A	A	Y	G	L	T	A	B	B	C	G	Y	T	P	Y
R	Q	B	O	M	Y	P	R	V	L	X	E	C	K	N	Y
E	P	I	U	E	T	S	H	A	R	K	E	K	R	T	E
T	Z	R	N	M	A	L	A	I	N	E	A	G	L	E	K
T	E	D	G	U	T	T	R	O	N	G	A	D	K	E	R
U	L	L	I	X	C	K	M	O	K	O	L	E	S	O	U
B	X	U	R	B	L	A	C	K	B	I	R	D	E	L	T

1. ______________
2. ______________
3. ______________
4. ______________
5. ______________
6. ______________
7. ______________
8. ______________
9. ______________

14 Memory test

Without looking at the text in your book, how many items can you name that are washed up on Kamilo Beach?

____

____

→ pages 50–51

What do you remember?

wiederverwendbar • Baumwoll- • biologisch abbaubar • sich riesig freuen (über) • Rede • Gefühl • verschmutzen • Sauerstoff • verschmutzen • Geschwindigkeit, Tempo • abbauen, zerfallen • Wahnsinn, Irrsinn • Redner/-in • besorgt um etw. sein • gefühlsbetont • Wiederholung

In an interview a year after Modbury became the first plastic bag free town in the UK, several traders said they were ______________ with the town's attempts. "By encouraging customers to use ______________ ______________ bags and ______________ bags, we are helping people not to ______________ and ______________ both the land and the sea," said one trader. Another ______________, who obviously ______________ very strongly about the subject, showed a great deal of ______________ as he gave a ______________ talking of the ______________ of the ______________ at which humans are polluting the earth. "The environment can be a very ______________ topic," he said, "but it is a topic we cannot simply ignore. The earth's oceans are the lungs of the earth and give us much more ______________ than the rainforests; we cannot continue to abuse them as we have done. ______________ of previous mistakes is not acceptable. We have a duty to do the right thing and use materials which will ______________ quickly and naturally."

15 Word pairs

Match the verbs with the right prepositions. Then write one sentence for each word pair.

to be aware • to appeal • to be surrounded • to feel strongly • to be thrilled • to raise awareness • to clear • to campaign

by • about • up • with • of (2x) • for • to

1. ______________
2. ______________
3. ______________
4. ______________
5. ______________
6. ______________
7. ______________
8. ______________

16 Find the missing word

1. researcher – research • speaker – ______________
2. ignorance – ignorant • emotion – ______________
3. dog – puppy • seabird – ______________
4. hair – comb • lips – ______________
5. poison – poisonous • toxin – ______________
6. to empty – to fill up • to go down – ______________

→ pages 52–54

What do you remember?

züchten • seinen Lebensunterhalt bestreiten • spektakulär – Umgebung • Abendessen • bestehen (auf) • Truthahn • Semesterferien • Farm • Wiese, Viehweide • streicheln • Stolz • pusten, blasen • Ofenkartoffeln • bohren • Schinken

In Nicholas Evans' novel, Abbie Cooper stays at a ranch in Montana called 'The Divide'. There she meets Ty Hawkins, who is working on the ranch during his ______________. When Ty invites Abbie to visit his parents' ______________ in Wyoming, she learns about the problems of some families who ______________ a ______________ from ______________ horses, and whose life-style is now at risk from companies ______________ for gas on their land.

Arriving in the dark at the Hawkins' ranch, a fantastic ______________ is waiting for Ty and Abbie: cold ______________ and ______________ and ______________. Ty's parents ______________ that they eat as much as they can while they listen to their son with obvious ______________.

The next day, Abbie admires the ______________ ______________ when Ty and his father Ray take her to a ______________ to see some colts. Abbie copies Ty's father, and the horses let her ______________ them and ______________ into their noses.

17 Word formation

Change the words given to the form in brackets.

1. to insist ➜ (adjective) ______________
2. distance ➜ (adjective) ______________
3. to drive ➜ (noun) ______________
4. reference ➜ (verb) ______________
5. proud ➜ (noun) ______________
6. lease ➜ (verb) ______________
7. to characterize ➜ (noun) ______________
8. to wonder ➜ (adjective) ______________
9. to drill ➜ (noun) ______________
10. to create ➜ (noun) ______________

18 Synonyms

Replace the marked words with words which have the same or a very similar meaning.

1. Nicholas Evans began his **working life** (➜ ______________) as a journalist.
2. The **part** (➜ ______________) of his novel *The Divide* describes a trip by two young people to a **farm** (➜ ______________) in Wyoming during their college **holidays** (➜ ______________).
3. If the car breaks down on the way, I can help you to **mend** (➜ ______________) it.
4. Today a lot of cheap products are **brought in** (➜ ______________) which is bad for our local trade.
5. Don't put me on your list. I don't have time **anyway** (➜ ______________).
6. Suddenly they saw a person on the road **in front of** (➜ ______________) them.

→ pages 52–54

What do you remember?

Zeitraum • unterirdisch • Leute • Thema, Angelegenheit • Pacht • verwirrt • Bohren • Abbaurechte • was auch immer, egal was • Brief, Schreiben • (ver)pachten • eindringen • Methan • eingeschlossen werden • so genannte/-r/-s • untersuchen, überprüfen • in letzter Zeit, kürzlich

At lunch, Ty's mother suddenly gets serious and both Ty and Abbie are ______________ at first. When she explains her problem, Abbie feels she is ______________ on a private family ______________. "We've received a ______________ from the government explaining that we only own the surface rights to our land. It seems the government has always owned the ______________ and ______________ has started to ______________ them to companies which have found a cheap way of ______________ for ______________ gas. Apparently the land here is full of it; the gas ______________ in the coal seams ______________."

Ty's father continues: "Once a company has the ______________ for a ______________, they can start to ______________ the land for gas." He explains that the drilling companies offer the ranch owners a ______________ 'surface damage agreement' but he says that ______________ the ranchers do, the companies have the right to go ahead and drill anyway.

19 Say it in a different way

Use the words on the right to say the sentences in a different way.

1. Salt water goes all over the land and everything dies. **to flood**

   ____

2. People are of the opinion that drilling is good for the town. **to benefit**

   ____

3. Some of the machines have been working for many years. **to function**

   ____

4. When we arrived, there wasn't anyone in the restaurant. **deserted**

   ____

5. Sometimes it is difficult to describe the characters of the protagonists in a story. **to characterize**

   ____

20 Describing landscapes and the natural world

Find words from the text that can help you to describe landscapes and the natural world.

1. **adjectives:** ______________________________
2. **nouns:** ______________________________

→ pages 52–54

What do you remember?

Salz • aufbrechen, sich aufmachen • Fahrt • genau genommen • weiterfahren • abbiegen von • Steine • entfernen • (Erd-)Boden, Erde • Mengen • überschwemmen • einzig, einzeln • Lebewesen • auslaufen, undicht sein

Ty wants to show Abbie what effect the drilling has on the landscape and so ______________ the highway before the two friends ______________ back to The Divide. On the ______________ ahead, two giant excavators ______________ huge ______________ of earth and ______________ . "Drilling into the coal seams has a terrible effect on the land and its wildlife," explains Ty. "Huge amounts of water are released which ______________ the land, but because the water is ______________ water, not a ______________ fish can survive in the ponds here. Even when the holes are lined with plastic, they ______________ , and no one does anything about it!" Abbie is shocked and sad to see how the beautiful land has been affected.

Later on their ______________ back to The Divide, Abbie thinks about the day's experiences, the beauty of the land, and the wonderful ______________ she has come across. Somehow this does not count much in the thoughts of those wanting to drill for gas. ______________ , maybe it doesn't count at all. "I don't understand why folk are letting them do this," she says to Ty as they ______________ further.

21 Prepositions

Which preposition do you need to add to the second infinitive to give it a similar meaning to the first infinitive?

1. to leave • to set ______________
2. to find • to come ______________
3. to arrive • to turn ______________
4. to begin to cry • to break ______________
5. to clean • to clear ______________
6. to ascend • to go ______________

22 Odd word out

Which word does not fit? Cross it out and explain why.

1. turkey • ham • horse • chicken

   ______________ does not fit because ______________

2. wondrous • spectacular • deserted • heavenly

   ____

3. methane • salt • oxygen • carbon dioxide

   ____

4. letter • book • layer • paper

   ____

→ pages 52–54

What do you remember?

reparieren • funktionieren • austrocknen • Gasbohrarbeiter • verlassen • noch nicht • Arbeitskräfte • jmdm./etw. zugutekommen • Abmachung, Übereinkunft • (*hier:*) mitbringen, importieren

Ty's face becomes sadder as they pass ranches ______________ by their owners. "A lot of people don't want this to happen," Ty replies, "but other people do. For them, it's a good ______________ because they think it will ______________ the town by bringing in business to their stores and new jobs. Only it doesn't work like that – the companies often ______________ their own ______________ force. It's ______________ happening in Montana, but … The ______________ really don't care if the landscape is ruined or the wells ______________ after ______________ well for years. Most of the companies don't make any attempt to ______________ things; all they are interested in is making money as quickly as possible."

23 A puzzle: Verbs

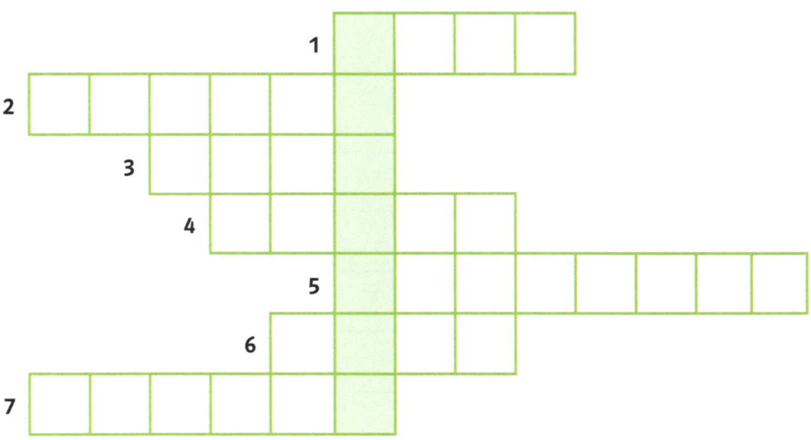

1. to take air into your body and then let it out again
2. to move your hand gently over something
3. to go somewhere in order to be with someone or do something with them
4. to keep animals or plants in order to produce babies or new plants
5. to work in the correct way
6. to breathe out making a loud sound, especially because you are bored, disappointed, tired etc.
7. to demand that something should happen

Solution: ______________________________

24 Find the missing word

1. painting – art • book – ______________
2. ahead of – behind • ______________ – back
3. recently – lately • confused – ______________
4. to stroke – hand • ______________ – mouth
5. benefit – advantage • to rent – ______________
6. article – newspaper • ______________ – novel

→ pages 52–54

What do you remember?

vor • so aussehen als ob • Tropfen • Front- – Windschutzscheibe • charakterisieren • informell • Kneipenbesitzer • bleibend • (Rechts-/Staats-)Anwälte • Literatur

"How would you ______ the protest against the drilling?" Abbie asks, looking ______ of her as large ______ of rain hit the ______ ______.

"Well, it's very widespread," Ty replies, "there has been a formal protest from some ______, and a great deal of ______ protesting from trades folk such as ______ and shop traders. Recently they have been giving out information leaflets and ______ to all their customers in an attempt to raise awareness. Whether they will have a ______ impact is difficult to say. The drilling companies ______ to carry on whatever."

25 Words and their definitions

a) *Find the words that are described by the following definitions.*

1. a light evening meal: ______
2. a vegetable grown in the ground which is often fried or baked: ______
3. cooked cold meat: ______
4. a field of grass: ______
5. a person employed as a lawyer in America: ______
6. the glass which protects the driver at the front of a car: ______
7. the person who owns a bar: ______

b) *Write your own definition for the following words.*

1. **extract:** ______
2. **gas driller:** ______
3. **setting:** ______

26 Opposites

Find the opposites of the following words.

1. to break • ______
2. to stop • ______
3. to lift • ______
4. full of people • ______
5. near • ______
6. to arrive • ______
7. following • ______
8. past • ______
9. behind • ______
10. formal • ______

→ page 55

What do you remember?

Verfasser/-in • Mit- • Jurymitglied • Debatte • abwägen • reduzieren, verringern • Kohlenstoff • Kernenergie • dringend • (ver)meiden – predigen, propagieren • selten • Oscar-gekrönt • effektiv, nachhaltig

__________ environmental films are __________ made. The Turin environmental film festival helps to make sure good films receive recognition.

This year, in my role as a __________ for a well-known newspaper, I was asked to be a __________ at the Turin festival. Before making any decisions, we had to have a __________ on the best features of each film and __________ how __________ the films had been. It was rare that I agreed entirely with my __________ jury members. Generally speaking, I look for films where the message is clear but which try to __________ __________ to its viewers, however __________ the message might be. Last year's film winner was *The nuclear comeback*, which weighed up the pros and cons of __________ and showed very effectively how urgent it is to __________ our __________ dioxide emissions.

27 Word formation

Change the words given to the form in brackets.

1. drama → (verb) __________
2. power → (adjective) __________
3. human → (noun) __________
4. to write → (noun) __________
5. to imagine → (noun) __________
6. effect → (adjective) __________
7. to urge → (adjective) __________
8. to weigh up → (noun) __________

28 How does the text say it?

Fill in the words that are used on the Film page without looking at the text again.

1. Earlier this week I spent a long lunch in Turin with **other** (→ __________) jury members […]. (l. 2)
2. After three hours of **discussion** (→ __________) we finally decided on a winner. (l. 5)
3. Ask any cinema-goer to name their favourite environmental film, and you probably **won't get** (→ __________) much further than *An inconvenient truth* […]. (l. 19)
4. Hollywood has also **made into a film** (→ __________) the real-life stories of those who have fought for environmental causes […]. (l. 40)
5. *Koyaanisqatsi* is a haunting meditation on the relationship between **people** (→ __________), technology and the natural environment. (l. 50)
6. It combines striking **pictures** (→ __________) with a mind-changing message. (l. 52)

→ page 55

What do you remember?

mit großem Budget • Animationen; Zeichentrickfilme • Verurteilung • weltweit • Bestände • verfilmen • Menschheit • authentisch • Überbevölkerung • beeindruckend • Veröffentlichungen • kombinieren, verbinden • bemerkenswert, auffallend – Bilder, Bildsprache • angeben, prahlen • Filmgattungen

"What ______________ are suitable for promoting environmental issues?" a friend asked recently. "That's a difficult question," I replied. "They can be science fiction, ______________, ______________ stories … a number of types really. ______________ movies have been very effective recently in getting over really ______________ messages. They have ______________ environmental issues and the future of ______________ through very ______________ ______________. One of the most celebrated ______________ I have seen recently ______________ how ______________ fish ______________ have been affected by over-fishing and pollution. Another very good film provided a ______________ of western life-style and looked at the environmental effects of ______________ on the earth's resources. I can send you a list of some of the best movies if you like."

"That would be great – I can't ______________ much knowledge of films and it would be good to develop a new interest."

29 Word search: Film words

Find ten words you can use to talk about films and translate them into German. The words go →, ↓, ↑, ←, ↗ and ↖.

T	F	I	L	M	M	A	K	E	R	N	H	C	D	T	R
E	D	X	R	O	T	F	L	U	O	L	A	E	R	B	E
F	A	Y	R	E	G	A	M	I	B	R	G	G	A	I	T
I	L	K	S	M	M	P	T	V	L	E	U	A	M	G	I
L	P	W	X	E	E	A	H	A	R	L	E	S	A	B	R
L	E	R	L	C	M	T	A	I	G	E	A	S	T	U	W
A	E	R	I	I	S	T	R	T	N	A	A	E	I	D	K
E	L	G	N	I	K	I	R	T	S	S	L	M	S	G	R
R	S	A	O	E	X	A	C	K	B	E	R	D	E	E	U
S	K	W	R	M	G	T	M	P	L	X	S	R	F	T	L

1. ______________
2. ______________
3. ______________
4. ______________
5. ______________
6. ______________
7. ______________
8. ______________
8. ______________
10. ______________

→ pages 56–57

What do you remember?

Fußabdruck • beinhalten, einschließen • Fleischwurst • laut, gemäß • wann immer • Milchprodukte • Haushalt • ernten • zu dem Ergebnis kommen • Transport • verursachen, ausmachen • Treibhausgas • als Ergebnis von • Verbrauch, Konsum • landwirtschaftlich, Agrar- • (*hier:*) anbauen • verantwortlich

The writer Sage Van Wing tries to ______________ locally grown products in her diet ______________ she can, in an attempt to minimise her carbon ______________ .

She regularly goes to a nearby farmers' market to buy vegetables or cheese, and when she wants meat, such as ______________ , she goes to her local butcher's.

______________ the researcher Christopher Weber however, eating less red meat and ______________ can be a more effective way of reducing your carbon footprint than buying local food. Christopher Weber ______________ in his research study that ______________ only ______________ 11% of the greenhouse gases generated annually by an average US ______________ as a ______________ of food ______________ . The ______________ and industrial practices required to ______________ and to ______________ food are ______________ for much of our ______________ emissions.

30 Memory test

Answer the following questions without looking at the text in your books.

1. What five ingredients does Sage Van Wing include in her lunch on a typical spring day?

   ____

2. Replacing red meat and dairy products with what three ingredients for one day per week reduces emissions equal to 760 miles per year of driving? ______________________________

3. Switching to what food type one day per week cuts the equivalent of driving 1,160 miles per year?

   ____

31 Noun suffixes

Choose the right suffix to make nouns from these words. Complete the grid.

responsible • to produce • influential • to repeat • mad • to measure • to reduce • to differ • to pollute • to emit

-ity	-ness	-tion / -sion	-ment	-ance / -ence

→ pages 56–57

What do you remember?

ausmachen, betragen • gesamt, Gesamt- • Ernährung • vergleichsweise, verhältnismäßig • Abnahme, Reduzierung • einige, verschiedene • Studien, Untersuchungen • energieeffizient • Tomaten • Kopfsalat • beheizt – Treibhäuser • Bauern • Herstellung

"The ______ greenhouse gas emissions behind our carbon footprints are made up of a complex number of factors," said an environmental researcher in a television interview yesterday. "Even if we changed to a completely local ______, this might only ______ a ______ small ______ in our greenhouse gas emissions. ______ recent ______ have shown that buying locally grown food produced in ______ ______ by ______ in countries with a cooler climate, such as the UK, can be less ______ than buying ______ and ______ from a warmer country, such as Spain, where heated greenhouses are not required for effective ______."

32 Word formation

Change the words given to the form in brackets.

1. to reduce → (noun) ______
2. influence → (adjective) ______
3. grower → (verb) ______
4. product → (verb) ______
5. consumer → (noun) ______
6. matter → (verb) ______
7. transport → (verb) ______
8. special → (noun) ______
9. to offend → (noun) ______
10. short → (noun) ______

33 Spot the mistakes

Find one mistake in each sentence and correct them.

1. I love the real English breakfast – baked beans, bacon, mushrooms and tomatos.
2. The answers to your questions are relative difficult.
3. Do you know the average consumption of meat per head in your country?
4. Less animals would have to die if more people replaced meat for vegetables.

34 Units of measurement

Choose an appropriate word from the box to complete the weights or measures below.

kilogram • gram • millilitre • pint • bottle • slice

1. a ______ of bread
2. 150 ______ of butter
3. a ______ of milk
4. 200 ______ of water
5. a ______ of beer
6. one ______ of potatoes

→ pages 56–57

What do you remember?

Lebensmittel • ethisch, moralisch • Verbraucher, Konsumenten • Rindfleisch • Gewohnheiten • Elektrogeräte • Liter • bewerten, auswerten • Hemd, Shirt • (Taschen-)Rechner • Fall • (*hier:*) berücksichtigen • Scheibe • Wein • Pint • umwandeln in

__________ wishing to change their buying __________ by shopping in a more __________ way need to know a lot about each product, for example, their 'water footprint'. The 'water footprint' tells us the amount of water that has been used in the manufacture of a product. Popular goods such as __________, __________ and clothes can now be __________ according to their water footprint using a water footprint __________.
In each __________, the calculation __________ both the manufacture and the transport of the goods.
A __________ of white bread has a water footprint of 40 __________, a glass of __________ 120 litres, and a cotton __________ 2,700 litres. The water footprint of beef and dairy products is also a lot higher than many people expect: for example, a __________ of milk has a water footprint of 1,760 litres, just one kilogram of cheese has a footprint of 5,000 litres, and one kilogram of __________ has a water footprint of 15,500 litres! Knowing the last figure alone should be enough to __________ everyone __________ a vegetarian!

35 A puzzle: Food

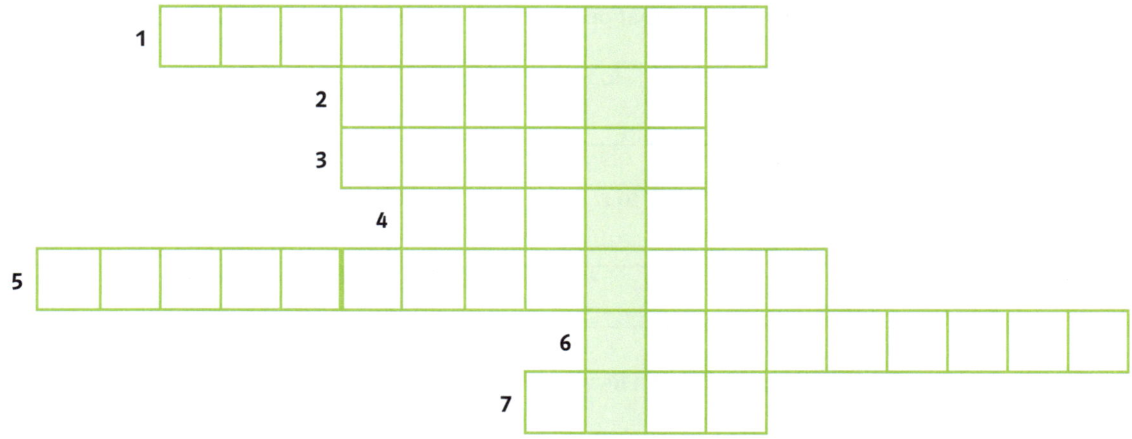

1. plants that are eaten raw or cooked, such as carrots or beans
2. a powder that is used to add a hot taste to food
3. a round soft red fruit eaten raw or cooked as a vegetable
4. an Italian food made from flour, eggs, and water and cut into different shapes
5. products which are made from milk
6. a powder or liquid, such as salt or ketchup, that you use to give a special taste to food
7. the meat from a cow

Solution: ____________________

→ pages 56–57

What do you remember?

Weizen • weltweit • Übeltäter/-in • Kubikmeter • pro Kopf • Verschwendung • kompliziert – Berechnungen • sehr daran interessiert sein, etw. zu tun • vermindern, minimieren • wiederverwerten, recyceln • Dünger • obwohl

__________ water covers much of our planet, it is still very precious.

A __________ league table of the water footprints of different countries shows the US to be the main __________ with a water footprint of almost 2,500 __________ per year __________. Italy is a close second.

The water footprint of important foods such as __________ or meat is much greater in general than that of products such as apples and coffee. This makes it hard to work out how to __________ your water footprint. However, consumers who are __________ reduce their water __________ do not have to carry out __________ __________ if they live by one very simple rule: always __________. This avoids the manufacture of completely new products. In the case of a cotton shirt this would mean less water being used to irrigate and wash away __________ used in the growing of the cotton, for example.

36 Words and their definitions

Complete the words.

1. the effect or influence that an event, a situation etc. has on somebody or something: i __________
2. a point (thing, person or situation, for example) that people concentrate on: f __________
3. to start using something instead of another thing: to r __________
4. to reduce something: to c __________
5. to continue to be in the same state or condition: to r __________
6. to have an influence on something: to a __________
7. when something is not in its usual place: to b __________
8. products often used by farmers to raise production levels: f __________
9. too little water: w __________

37 Find the missing word

1. tomato – vegetable • milk – __________
2. spaghetti – pasta • __________ – grain
3. pork – pig • __________ – cow
4. company – boss • meeting – __________
5. to grow – grower • to consume – __________
6. millimetre – metre • __________ – litre
7. piece – cake • __________ – bread
8. one – once • two – __________

→ pages 58–61

What do you remember?

Kilogramm • Maß-, Größeneinheiten • Quadratmeilen • Kilometer • Volumen • Länge; (*hier:*) Dauer • existieren • nicht- • Entsprechung, Äquivalent

______________ in the US and the UK may be expressed in standard metric form or ______________-metric form. Examples of the non-metric measurements are often found in recipes, for example, where books may refer to 'ounces' and 'pounds' instead of grams and ______________. Similarly, whereas many countries express distance in ______________, in the US and the UK, distances are shown in 'miles' and area in '______________'. ______________ is expressed in metric measurements such as litres, or non-metric measurements such as pints and gallons.

In the US non-metric units of measurement are much more common than in the UK, where metric measurements are more often used in line with the rest of the European continent. Many older people in the UK, however, still refer to non-metric units of measurement and are not fully familiar with the ______________ metric measurements which are now ______________, particularly those of ______________ and weight.

38 Odd word out

Which word does not fit? Cross it out and explain why.

1. ounce • gallon • litre • inch

   ______________ does not fit because ______________

2. by air • by chance • by sea • by foot

   ____

3. nitrogen • carbon dioxide • gasoline • oxygen

   ____

4. to calculate • to multiply • to count • to report

   ____

39 Prepositions

Fill in the missing prepositions.

1. The majority ______ people at the demonstration remained peaceful.
2. It's fun to dress ______ before you go to a party.
3. According ______ a recent study a high number of teenagers are environmentally aware.
4. Global warming means that there is a worldwide rise ______ temperature.
5. Let's vote ______ the suggestions for our next class trip.
6. I'm scared to take the plane. Can we go ______ sea?

→ pages 58–61

What do you remember?

Unze • Zoll • Gallonen • Benzin • Faktoren, Gesichtspunkte • (be)rechnen • Mehrheit • Kohlestoffeinheiten • hypothetisch • Möglichkeit • neutral

Listeners to last night's radio show were asked to complete the missing words in the following questions or statements on non-metric measurements: **1)** I'll have a 14 ______ steak, please, with mushrooms. **2)** How many '______' are there in a 'foot'? **3)** ______ may be bought in gallons at a garage or service station. **4)** The lake held several thousands of ______ of water.

In the programme following this quiz, the presenter talked about the ______ which affect how environmentally friendly journeys are. She also explained how you can ______ the ______ for different journeys. Finally she compared the carbon units for a ______ journey from London to Naples in Italy when travelling by land, air and sea. A recent survey has shown that the ______ of people think travelling by train would be more environmentally friendly than travelling by car, but this is not the case. Actually, travelling by horse would be the best ______, but still not carbon ______, and travelling by car would be the next best choice.

40 Mixed bag

Fill in the missing word(s) in each sentence.

1. Phil is doing a 25 ______ run next week.
2. The area of rainforest destroyed each year is 63,000 ______.
3. 200 ______ of nitrogen is added to the land for every metric tonne of cotton harvested.
4. The predicted ______ by the end of the 21st century is 6 °C.
5. 'km' is the ______ for the word 'kilometre'.
6. 18 kilograms of methane is ______ 378 CU.
7. The earth has been ______ for 4.6 billion years.
8. The average ______ of water used ______ a toilet is 7 litres.

41 Word formation

Change the words given to the form in brackets.

1. to cut → (noun) ______
2. long → (noun) ______
3. emission → (verb) ______
4. allergy → (adjective) ______
5. ill → (noun) ______
6. major → (noun) ______
7. consideration → (verb) ______
8. to calculate → (noun) ______

→ pages 58–61

What do you remember?

Technologie • das Blatt wenden • verloren sein, verwirrt sein • Technologie • Reichtum, Wohlstand • eine grundlegende Veränderung • jmdn. zum Nachdenken bringen • (*hier:* Verantwortung) • ein Tropfen auf den heißen Stein • Ärger machen, für Aufruhr sorgen

Idioms are made up of groups of words which have a particular meaning when used together. An example of this is '__________' which has nothing to do with nuts or shells but which means that you express an idea in only a few words. This idiom is used as a heading for a report illustrating the number of carbon units emitted by five different forms of transport: car, train, plane, __________ and horse. By __________ different figures together, the researchers found that a horse would produce the lowest number of carbon units, followed by the car, the train, the plane and the cruise liner. Speaking of cruise liners, there are many idioms which have the sea as their origin, including 'a __________', 'a drop __________', 'to be __________', 'to turn __________' and 'to __________'. A recent campaign by a group of environmental protesters asked its members to produce posters using such idioms in order to make __________ about the use of modern __________, the environmental cost of economic __________ and whether we have a __________ to __________ as many of our products as possible.

42 Synonyms

Find synonyms for the following words.

1. to discover • __________
2. wealth • __________
3. possibility • __________
4. less than half • __________
5. pay • __________
6. to cause • __________
7. although • __________
8. per person • __________
9. to think about • __________
10. painful • __________

43 Idioms

a) *Underline the right explanations for the following idioms.*

1. a) to be confused b) to be lost c) to be wet — **to be all at sea**
2. a) a small change b) a huge change c) quite a big change — **a sea change**
3. a) something kept in a nutshell b) something very small c) something explained — **in a nutshell**

b) *Use one of the idioms above to complete the following sentences.*

1. It's a little hard to explain, but __________, this is what it means: … .
2. I don't know what I'm doing today. I'm __________!
3. Consumer habits won't change if there is not __________ in thinking on environmental issues.

→ pages 58-61

What do you remember?

Wange • Ell(en)bogen • Handgelenk • Daumen • Fußgelenk/-knöchel • Ferse • (Haut-)Ausschlag • -...schmerz(en) • Allergie (gegen) • schmerzhaft, wund • verstauchen • Schnittwunden • Prellungen, blaue Flecken

"How's Jake after his accident? I heard he'd broken his arm in two places – his ______________ and his ______________."

"No, that was Pete; he ended up with a broken ______________ too, on his left hand. Jake just ______________ his ______________ and hurt his ______________. He has lots of ______________ and ______________ on his face, too, though – his ______________ looks swollen. I think he had a head ______________ for a couple of days."

"Well, they were lucky not to be more seriously hurt. How did your sister enjoy her holiday, by the way?"

"That was a bit of a disaster, too! She developed an ______________ to something she ate and came out in a really bad ______________. She's back now, but she's off work as she has a very bad ______________ throat."

44 A puzzle: At the doctor's

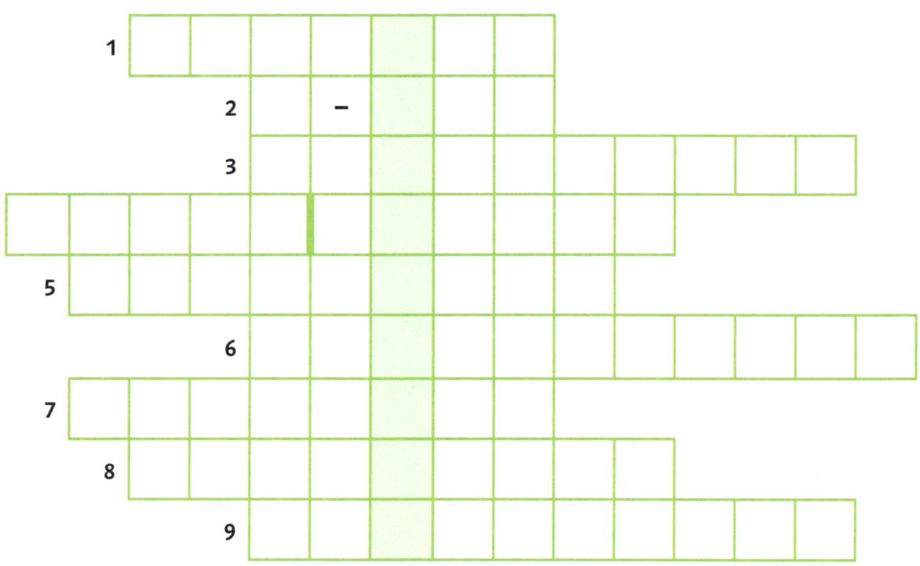

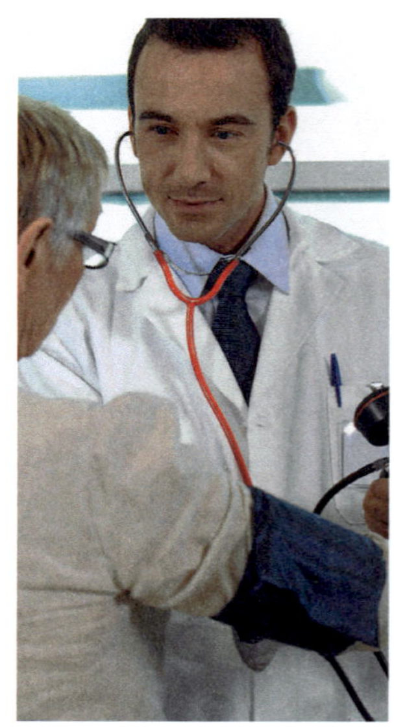

1. something wrong with your body which shows that you have a particular illness
2. to photograph the inside of someone's body
3. a doctor who knows more about one particular type of illness or treatment than other doctors
4. what a doctor takes from your body to examine or test
5. doctors give these – they put a drug into someone's body using a needle
6. when you want to try an alternative treatment, you can take … drugs
7. a soft cream that you rub into your skin, especially as a medical treatment
8. the process of discovering exactly what is wrong with someone
9. a drug that is used to kill bacteria and cure infections

Solution: ______________________________

→ pages 58–61

What do you remember?

beißen • verheilen • geschwollen • entzündet • Durchfall • Infekt(ion) • Heuschnupfen • Apotheke • verstopft sein • stechen • Tabletten • Nebenwirkungen

"Good morning, Mrs Jones. What's the problem?"

"Three things, doctor. I was ______________ or ______________ by something in Australia recently, and my ankle has become very ______________ ; it's almost twice the size of my other one. I went to the ______________ for advice, but nothing really helped."

"Yes, it does look very ______________ . I'll write you a prescription for some ______________ which should treat the problem; they won't have any ______________ , and your leg will ______________ inside a week, hopefully. What are the other two things bothering you?"

"I also developed ______________ and my stomach is still hurting badly. My partner had an ______________ , and I think I must have caught it from him. The last thing is my nose – it's always ______________ at night and then it runs a lot during the day; I don't know if I have a form of ______________ , maybe."

"Well, let's take the stomach problem first …"

45 Talking about your body

a) *Name the part of the body being described below.*

1. the part between your hand and arm ______________
2. between the upper and the lower arm ______________
3. one on each side of your face ______________
4. in between the leg and the foot ______________
5. used like a finger; one on each hand ______________

Can you name five other body parts?

____

____

b) *Find a better word or phrase for these explanations.*

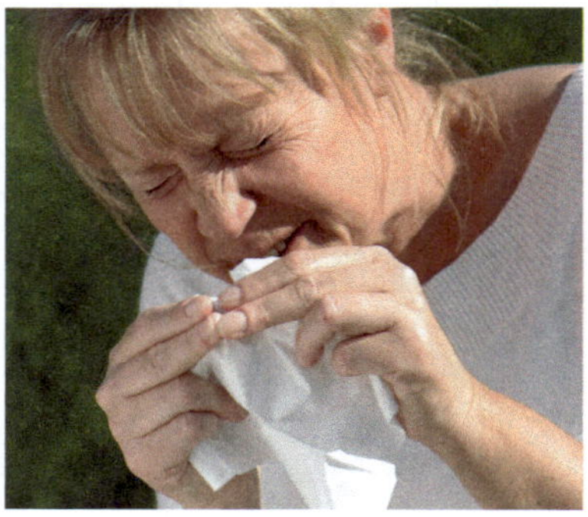

1. bad effects of a medicine ______________
2. to get better (for example, cuts) ______________
3. an allergy to plants or flowers ______________
4. illness which causes you to go to the toilet a lot ______________
5. swollen and red ______________

46 Words and their definitions: Environmental issues

a) *Match the words from the box with the right definitions.*

acid rain • chemical • toxin • recycling plant • climate • ozone layer • reusable • wastage • methane • greenhouse gas

1.		a gas that you cannot see or smell, which can be burned to give heat
2.		a place where garbage is recycled
3.		rain that can damage the environment, caused by chemicals in the air
4.		the typical weather conditions in a particular area
5.		a layer of gases in the sky
6.		a poisonous substance that can kill you or make you sick
7.		when something is lost or destroyed, especially in a way that is not useful
8.		a gas that is said to trap heat above the Earth
9.		when you can use something more than once
10.		a substance used in chemistry or produced by a chemical process

b) *Write down your own definition for the following words.*

1. **overpopulation:** ____________________
2. **energy efficient:** ____________________
3. **global warming:** ____________________

47 A quiz

How many of the following quiz questions can you answer correctly without looking at your textbook? Use vocabulary from Topic 3 to give the answers.

1. What is the name (4 words) of a famous international pressure group that campaigns to protect the environment?

   ____

2. Germany produces 3 % of what? ____________________
3. What name (3 words) is given to a type of living which creates a huge amount of rubbish and waste?

   ____

4. What does it take the earth 3 million years to do? ____________________
5. What is released out of the earth when drilling for gas takes place? (2 word noun)

   ____

6. Can you name a unit of measurement for each of the following ?

   a) liquid ____________________ c) distance ____________________

   b) temperature ____________________ d) weight ____________________

7. What is 21 times more powerful a greenhouse gas than CO_2? ____________________
8. What do you call conversations with little meaning? ____________________
9. What might a doctor give you to fight off infection? ____________________

Topic 4 South Africa

→ pages 66–67

What do you remember?

Politik • seit dann • Wahrzeichen • Industriezweig • Produzent • weitgehend • jmdn. unterdrücken • Rassentrennung • die Mehrheit von • Kampf • international • Diamanten • Tourismus • unterschiedlich – Landschaft • eine Vielzahl von • Finanzsektor

Before 1994, when South Africa had its first democratic election, ______________ South Africans had been ______________ for years by the country's ______________ of ______________ . At last their ______________ was over. Nelson Mandela became the country's first black president, and ______________ South Africa has become ______________ accepted by the ______________ community. South Africa has always been, and still is, a leading ______________ of ______________ and gold. The ______________ attracts a lot of foreign investment, and South Africa is a leading exporter of ______________ products. In the last twenty years, ______________ has also become an important ______________ . People from all over the world want to visit the famous ______________ and enjoy the ______________ ______________ .

1 Word formation

Change the words given to the form in brackets.

1. descended from → (noun) ______________
2. symbol → (verb) ______________
3. struggle → (verb) ______________
4. diversity → (adjective) ______________
5. to produce → (noun) ______________
6. wealth → (adjective) ______________
7. industrial → (noun) ______________
8. original → (noun) ______________
9. nature → (adjective) ______________
10. to believe → (noun) ______________

2 Synonyms

Replace the marked words with words which have the same or a very similar meaning.

1. The colour yellow in the flag **represents** (→ ______________) the country's mineral resources.
2. A lot of South Africans are very **rich** (→ ______________).
3. He works in the manufacturing **part** (→ ______________).
4. What are the country's **laws and regulations** (→ ______________) in terms of immigration?
5. The **largest number** (→ ______________) of South Africans are able to speak English.
6. For a long time, South Africa was dominated by people of Dutch **origin** (→ ______________).
7. Before Cape Town was founded by Dutch traders, indigenous **tribes** (→ ______________) had lived there.

→ pages 66–67

What do you remember?

überdenken • Townships • Machtübergabe • Afrikaans • Weltmeisterschaft • stehen für • Flagge • im Gegensatz zu – Niederländisch • südafrikanisch • niederländisch – Händler

One of the 11 official languages in South Africa is ______________ . It is not completely ______________ ______________ – from which it developed many years ago, when ______________ ______________ settled in South Africa. Because many black people living in ______________ were forced to use Afrikaans in schools, the language began to ______________ the power of the white ______________ government. Another symbol of the 'old South Africa' was the country's ______________ . The ______________ to the majority brought with it a chance to ______________ the design of the new country's flag, and the football ______________ in 2010 has helped to make this flag become well-known to the rest of the world.

3 Spot the mistakes

Find one mistake in each sentence and correct them.

1. What are your political believes? ______________
2. Singapore is a popular stayover point for travellers flying from Europe to Australia. ______________
3. Many people visit South Africa's national parks to view the fantastic night life. ______________
4. James is tall and quiet – completely unlikely his brother, who is short and loud. ______________

4 Prepositions

Fill in the missing prepositions.

1. Does this book belong ________ you?
2. My family is descended ________ French settlers.
3. Try to eat a variety ________ fruit and vegetables every day.
4. The country had a long struggle ________ independence.
5. My parents put a lot of pressure ________ me to study more next term.

5 Bits and pieces

Match the syllables from the boxes and form words with three syllables.

re- • coun- • act-

-sourc- • -iv- • -try- • -pub-

-es • -side • -lic • -ist

1. ______________
2. ______________
3. ______________
4. ______________

→ pages 66–67

What do you remember?

Minen • Republik • Zwischenstopp • verhandeln • finanziell • entweder … oder … • Radfahren • Gewürzstraße • Herstellung • Bodenschätze • Freiheitskämpfer

The countryside is flat, so it's perfect for ______________ .

He is completely bilingual, so you can speak to him ______________ in German ______________ in English.

Many of Britain's coal ______________ were closed long ago.

Brazil is rich in ______________ , for example diamonds.

South Africa became a ______________ in 1961.

The airport in Johannesburg is named after the great ______________ Oliver Tambo.

I was able to ______________ a very good deal on my new phone contract.

Britain was once a leader in car ______________ , but this is no longer the case.

In former times Cape town was a ______________ on the ______________ .

6 Say it in a different way

Fill in the missing word. The two sentences must have the same meaning.

1. Mr Parker, our new manager, has a lot of experience in business.

   → He has a lot of ______________ experience.

2. We were shocked to hear about the very rough treatment of some of the prisoners.

   → Some of the prisoners suffered ______________ treatment in prison.

3. London is a city of people from many different cultures.

   → London is a very ______________ city.

4. South Africa sells a lot of minerals, including gold and diamonds, to other countries.

   → South Africa ______________ gold and diamonds.

5. Nelson Mandela is a member of the Thembu tribe.

   → Nelson Mandela ______________ to the Thembu tribe.

6. He stands for the struggle for freedom in South Africa.

   → He ______________ the struggle for freedom in South Africa.

7. Every year a lot of tourists come to South Africa.

   → ______________ has became an important economic factor.

→ pages 68–69

What do you remember?

Festnahmen • Freiheitskämpfer • Gerichtsverfahren • Visionär • Nationengründer • Widerstand • gründen • politisch • zu etw. hingehen – Treffen • Verbot • im Untergrund • verbieten • Gefängnisstrafen

The African National Congress (ANC) is a ______________ party in South Africa. It was originally a black ______________ movement ______________ to lead the struggle against the government's policy of racial separation, known as Apartheid. The government put a ______________ on the ANC from 1960 to 1990 and the party's members were ______________ to ______________ ______________. During this time the ANC worked ______________. Nelson Mandela, who became the symbol of the anti-Apartheid movement, had to suffer several ______________ and ______________ in his life. In 1964 at the Rivonia ______________, he and other ______________ were sentenced to life imprisonment. In 1990 after 27 years in prison, he was finally freed. He led the country to democracy and become its first black president. He proved to be a true ______________ and ______________ – someone whose dream for a better future for all became an inspiration for others, and eventually, a reality.

7 Word pairs

Match the words to form common collocations (words that are usually used together). Then write a sentence with each of the words.

to write • to arrest • to be sentenced • to contain • to attend • to work • to be deprived	a criminal • a meeting • an autobiography • as a civil servant • of one's rights • to jail • useful information

1. ______________
2. ______________
3. ______________
4. ______________
5. ______________
6. ______________
7. ______________

8 Opposites

Find the opposites of the following words.

1. to import • ______________
2. majority • ______________
3. like • ______________
4. to import • ______________
5. to allow • ______________
6. poor • ______________
7. town • ______________
8. easy • ______________

→ pages 68–69

What do you remember?

Prozess • bestimmte/-r/-s • gleichzeitig • Heft • beeinträchtigen, sich auswirken auf • Massen- • Polizisten • Weg • arbeitslos • jährlich • verfolgen • erheben

In South Africa under Apartheid, a special ____________ tax was ____________ only on black people.

All the information you need is in the small ____________ you have been given.

It can be difficult to do several things ____________ .

The ____________ caught the criminal when he was just about to rob the bank.

The number of people who are ____________ has risen because of the financial crisis.

There was a ____________ protest by teachers about the pay cuts planned by the government.

The "____________ to freedom" in South Africa was a long and difficult ____________ .

In ____________ countries around the world, people are still ____________ for their opinions and beliefs.

How do you think the new law is going to ____________ you personally?

9 Synonyms

Replace the marked words with words which have the same or a similar meaning.

1. It is a very **difficult and complex process** (→ ____________).
2. At our school, jewellery is **banned** (→ ____________).
3. There are security checks to make sure passengers are not **carrying guns or knives** (→ ____________).
4. He had to pay a **certain amount of money** (→ ____________) because he had broken the law.
5. We all made an **attempt** to change our behaviour (→ ____________).
6. The criminal was given a **prison** sentence (→ ____________).

10 Words and their definitions

Complete the words.

1. someone who has clear ideas about the way something should be in the future: v ____________
2. money that you have to pay to a punishment: f ____________
3. when you are without a job: to b ____________
4. fighting against someone who is attacking you: r ____________
5. to treat someone cruelly or unfairly over a period of time: to p ____________
6. a book in which someone writes about his or her own life: to p ____________

→ pages 70

What do you remember?

Auszug • Phase • Würdigung • genau – sich an etw. erinnern • Strophe • veröffentlichen • sich weiterentwickeln • frühere/-r/-s • Dokumentation

The film *Invictus* was ________________ in 2009. It is a film based on a book called *Playing the Enemy*, which is a ________________ by reporter John Carlin and a ________________ of ________________ President Nelson Mandela's handling of the 1995 Rugby World Cup in South Africa. He used the event cleverly to help the country ________________ and become one nation. John Carlin interviewed the players on the South African rugby team, and also Mandela himself, and his book ________________ ________________ much of what happened in this ________________ of South African history. The name of the film is taken from a poem called Invictus, which is one of Nelson Mandela's favourite poems. The following lines are an ________________ from the last ________________ : *I am the master of my fate: I am the captain of my soul.*

11 Odd word out

Which word does not fit? Cross it out and explain why.

1. historian • republic • policeman • civil servant

   ________________ does not fit, because ________________

2. arrest • trial • jail sentence • industry

   ____

3. to oppress • to persecute • to deprive • to trace

   ____

4. trader • visionary • freedom-activist • freedom-fighter

   ____

5. Afrikaans • Germany • Netherlands • South Africa

   ____

12 Word families

Write the noun or verb forms for each word.

Noun	Verb
1. release	
2. accompaniment	
3.	to state
4.	to celebrate
5.	to fight
6.	to resist

→ pages 78–79

What do you remember?

Personal • Komfort • Wildreservat • sicherstellen • malerisch • Reiseziele • zu etw. gehören • Unterkunft • traditionell • Vielfalt • etw. einschließen, beinhalten • von … zu … reichen • übernachten • Tierarten • Safaris • großartig, überwältigend • Pflanzenwelt

One of the main tourist ______________ for visitors to South Africa is a visit to a ______________ . Kruger National Park ______________ the world's top parks. The huge ______________ of ______________ in the park ______________ that people on ______________ will see some or all of the 'big five' – which ______________ elephants, buffalos and lions. However, apart from the ______________ animals, the ______________ surroundings and the ______________ make Kruger Park one of the most popular landmarks on any trip to South Africa. There is a variety of ______________ in the Park, ______________ cheap to luxury hotels. You can ______________ in simple, ______________ housing, or in a more luxurious hotel, where the ______________ will make sure that you have every ______________ .

13 A puzzle: Words to do with wildlife

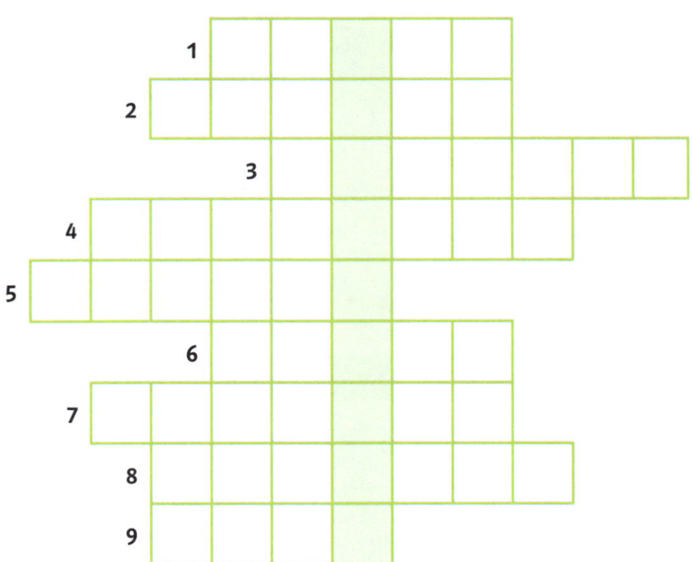

1. an animal with a long thin body and no legs
2. A lion is an example of a …
3. There are many different animal …
4. a very large grey animal
5. You should definitely go on a … when you go to South Africa.
6. A … belongs to the horse family.
7. The crocodile is a very dangerous …
8. a tall African animal with a very large neck and legs
9. a large animal of the cat family with gold-coloured fur

Solution: ______________________________

→ pages 78–79

What do you remember?

fast • jmdn. führen • Zivilisation • übertrieben • majestätisch • einheimisch • Ausgrabungsstätte

The springbok is a species which is ______________ to South Africa.

The 'Cradle of Humankind' is a famous ______________ in South Africa. Many people believe that we can trace back the origins of humankind to this particular place.

The sight of Table Mountain, which towers above the city of Cape Town, is truly ______________.

On our recent trip we were very lucky to be accompanied by a famous historian who taught us a lot about ancient ______________ as he ______________ us through the sites.

The travel text is too ______________, but at first I ______________ believed what it said.

14 Find the missing word

1. frog – amphibian • snake – ______________
2. Germany – German • Netherlands – ______________
3. ball – football • bike – ______________
4. book – autobiography • film – ______________
5. police – policeman • state – ______________
6. trade – trader • production – ______________

15 Noun suffixes

Choose the right suffix to make nouns from these words. Complete the grid.

civilize • diverse • document • enjoy • improve • major • meet • paint • select • vision

-ment	-ion	-ing	-ity	-ary

16 Choose the right word

Underline the correct word to complete the sentences.

1. There is a (fence • staff • phase) around the safari camp to keep the animals out.
2. The countryside is beautiful and (included • unspoilt • selected).
3. The guided tours (descend • release • depart) from here every hour.
4. The organisation was (established • preserved • ensured) to protect wildlife in Africa.
5. There has been a great (transition • comfort • improvement) in hotel standards since our last visit.

→ pages 78–79

What do you remember?

gründen • etw. bewahren, erhalten • Auswahl • unberührt • offene Savanne • Freude, Genuss • schützen • Malereien • beeindruckend – Naturreservat • Tierarten

Do you want a holiday unlike any other holiday you've ever had? Then come on safari in Kruger National Park! This ________ ________ was ________ in the last century to ________ wildlife. Thanks to their efforts, they have ensured that many species have been ________ In my opinion, nothing beats the ________ of standing on a hill outside your camp, looking at the ________ landscape of the ________ . You can not only enjoy a large ________ of wildlife safari tours, but you can also admire rock ________ and visit archaeological sites. So make the Kruger National Park your number one destination!

17 Odd word out

Which word does not fit? Cross it out and explain why.

1. mammal • zebra • reptile • amphibian

   ____

2. scenic • magnificent • impressive • brutal

   ____

3. booklet • excerpt • painting • autobiography

   ____

4. species • diversity • variety • selection

   ____

5. to protect • to etablish • to save • to preserve

   ____

18 Which word does not fit?

Cross out one word that cannot be used in these sentences.

1. We enjoyed staying in the (unspoilt • complicated • scenic) countryside.
2. That's a very (majestic • impressive • wealthy) painting.
3. The site must be preserved for its (archaeological • political • republic) importance.
4. The game reserve was (contained • formed • established) to protect the animals.
5. A historian will (accompany • guide • persecute) you through the site to help you learn about the ancient civilization that once lived there.

→ pages 80–83

What do you remember?

zurückgehen • jmdn. erziehen • Umweltschützer • Schlüssel • begrenzt • ermuntern • Elfenbein • Erhaltung • Heilmittel • Nachfrage • reduzieren • Gesundheitspflege • Töten • HIV • wahrscheinlich •

__________ is an important __________ issue in South Africa. The government is __________ medical researchers to make every effort to find a __________ .

In certain parts of the country, especially in the countryside, financial resources are __________ , and it isn't very __________ that the number of cases will be greatly __________ in the near future. However, in recent years the number of cases is __________ somewhat.

Another important issue in South Africa is the brutal __________ of elephants and rhinos to meet the __________ for __________ from international dealers. If people aren't __________ about the need for __________ , many species will simply die out.

So education is the __________ to improving the situation, __________ say.

19 A crossword

Complete the crossword.

Across	Down
3. a person who mends water pipes, for example	1. a medicine or medical treatment to make someone healthy again
6. to give someone the courage or confidence to do something	2. to make something smaller
7. a synonym for 'probably'	4. a situation in which people have the same rights
8. a person who makes things out of wood	5. to become less

→ pages 80–83

What do you remember?

etw. führen • Beschreibung • Koch • Grillparty • Doppelzimmer (mit zwei getrennten Betten) • benötigen • Frühstückspension • Aufenthaltsraum • mit Badezimmer • ausgestattet • gemütlich • Werbeanzeige

On our last trip to South Africa we stayed in very ______________________ accommodation in the countryside. It is actually a ______________________ which is ______________________ farmer in the area. We saw an ______________________ for it and the ______________________ sounded perfect. In addition to the comfortable ______________________, which has an ______________________ bathroom, there is also a ______________________ and a small kitchen, which is well-______________________ with all that is ______________________ for cooking. But if you prefer, the farmer, who is a very good ______________________, will prepare all your meals. And you can join the farmer's family for a ______________________, which is a traditional South African way of cooking over an open fire. You will really enjoy it!

20 Word search: Accommodation

Find ten words in the puzzle. Use every word in 3–5 sentences. The words go →, ↓, ↑, ←, ↗, ↓ and ↖.

D	A	S	I	N	G	L	E	V	C	T
O	A	X	I	E	B	L	L	S	O	I
U	D	W	W	I	G	U	Y	T	N	S
B	T	O	O	N	I	N	G	A	F	O
L	C	E	I	Z	S	G	U	R	I	P
E	N	S	U	I	T	E	G	O	R	E
N	O	I	T	P	E	C	E	R	L	D
P	X	C	W	C	O	N	F	I	R	M
D	T	B	W	G	N	I	K	O	O	B

____

____

____

____

____

____

____

____

____

21 Prepositions

Complete the sentences with the right preposition.

1. When I've finished my training, I'll take __________ my parents' restaurant.
2. I hope you weren't put __________ by the pictures of dead elephants. Do you still want to go to Africa?
3. The hotel is run __________ a couple from Germany.
4. Studying for my exams takes __________ most of my time at the moment.
5. Please take __________ your shoes when you enter the house.
6. If you go __________ working this hard, you'll be really tired in the end.

→ pages 80–83

What do you remember?

Doppel- • Buchungen • Reiseführer • Wäscherei • Kaution • Föhn • Hütte, kleines Haus • Rand (Währung in Südafrika) • Einzel- • drahtloses, lokales Netzwerk • Rezeption • Sterne • Tal

The three-__________ hotel is situated in a scenic __________ in a nature reserve.

Would you prefer a __________ or two __________ rooms?

Every room is equipped with __________, so you are welcome to use your laptop.

Please call the __________ if there are any problems with your room.

You can have your clothes washed in the __________. Our staff will take care of this.

We require a 25% __________ for all __________.

Every room is equipped with a radio, TV and __________.

Our safaris are run by very experienced __________.

If you prefer to cook your own meals, you may wish to book one of our __________ instead.

They cost 350 __________ each, and are suitable for up to four people.

22 Say it in a different way

Use the words and phrases on the right to replace the marked words in the sentences so that the meaning remains the same.

1. Barry **was in charge of** the kitchen in a big financial institution. He then **carried on that line of work** to become head chef of his own restaurant.

   to run | to go on

   ____

   ____

2. If it was **my decision only**, I would **start** an organisation to **teach** young people the importance of conservation.

   to establish | to educate

   ____

   ____

3. The **natural plant life** in the Cape is **nearly the same as** that of the Mediterranean.

   vegetation | similar to

   ____

   ____

4. To **ensure** your **reservation**, please pay a **small percentage of the total amount**.

   to secure | booking | deposit

   ____

   ____

   ____

23 Words and their definitions: Nature and economy

a) *Match the words from the box with the right definitions.*

amphibian • savannah • mine • unspoilt • valley • conservationist • wealthy • trader • zebra

1.		the area that lies at the bottom of and between mountains
2.		plants in general or plants which are found in a particular area
3.		a person who buys and sells goods
4.		a person who works to protect animals, plants etc.
5.		an animal that can live in water as well as on land
6.		another word for 'rich'
7.		a black and white striped animal
8.		not having been changed or damaged by people
9.		a large flat area of land covered with grass, which is found in hot countries
10.		a system of holes in the ground that people make to remove mineral resources

b) *Write down three more words from the lexical field together with their definitions.*

____

____

____

____

24 Choose the right word

Cross out the word that cannot be used to complete these sentences.

1. The World Cup Stadium is one of Durban's best-loved (landmarks • landscapes).
2. I'd love to see the animals in a (game reserve • safari).
3. The area is rich in (vegetation • wildlife) – we saw a lot of zebras, lion and elephants on our trip.
4. Kruger National Park does a lot of work in (conservationist • conservation).
5. Professor Willis is a historian who is studying findings at an important (archaeological site • natural resource).
6. South Africa is rich in (mineral • natural) resources such as water and trees.

Topic 5 Make a difference

→ pages 92–93

What do you remember?

Angriff • sich weigern • ziviler Ungehorsam • Gesellschaftskritiker • Philosophen • Steuer • Ziel • Verhalten • sich beteiligen an • gewaltfrei • rebellieren gegen • anerkennen • Vorgehensweise • Staatsbürger • sich schuldig machen

__________ is a difficult topic. Some people __________ to obey the law because they want to __________ things they feel are unfair. Many __________ those people's actions as an effective __________ while for others they are simply criminals. Can you really __________ a crime and be a good __________? Some __________ would say it depends on the reasons for your __________. If you don't pay your __________ because you want to keep your money, you are not a __________. You are just selfish. If you __________ violent activities, and plan an __________ on people to achieve a political __________, that is more than disobedience. Our heroes are often those who achieved change through __________ protest.

1 Odd word out

Which word does not fit? Cross it out and explain why.

1. philosopher • behaviour • biologist • preacher

   __________ does not fit because __________

2. ecological • international • tactic • major

   ____

3. antibiotic • cure • treatment • citizen

   ____

4. current • future • major • annual

   ____

2 Words and their definitions

Complete the definitions.

1. **social critic:** a person who __________
2. **goal:** describes something that __________
3. **ecological:** good for our __________
4. **preacher:** a person who __________
5. **biologist:** a person who __________

→ pages 92–93

What do you remember?

international • Heilmittel gegen • Entdeckung • Erwachsenenalter • Penicillin • antibiotisch • wie (zum Beispiel) • Biologen – starten • bedeutend • Todesurteil • Behandlung • seitdem

Not long ago many children never reached ______________ because diseases ______________ pneumonia were a ______________. Today the situation is completely different thanks to ______________ medicine and better food. ______________ Alexander Fleming's ______________ of ______________, we have had effective medical ______________ for bacterial illnesses. Of course, other types of illnesses still cannot be cured. ______________ teams of doctors and ______________ ______________ new projects every year, hoping to find a ______________ HIV or Alzheimer's disease, for example. ______________ discoveries have been made but there is still a lot of work to be done in the future.

3 Words and their definitions

Complete the words.

1. to give money or things, for example to a charity: to d ______________
2. to murder someone for political reasons: to a ______________
3. another word for 'yearly': a ______________
4. not future and not past: c ______________
5. not using physical force: n ______________
6. a kind of organisation that does not make a profit: f ______________

4 Mixed bag

Use the words from exercise 3 to complete the sentences.

1. ______________ protest can achieve a lot.
2. I don't think our ______________ leaders are good for the country.
3. He gave us £20,000 to start a ______________ for helping Ethiopian hospitals.
4. I want to ______________ some money but I don't know which charity is best.

5. We have an ______________ concert to raise money for the music school.
6. There are people who ______________ other people for money.

→ pages 92–93

What do you remember?

Diskriminierung • Budget • Bewusstsein • zukünftig • Vorreiter • Gründer • Gesundheitsversorgung • Einfluss • Afroamerikaner • spenden • ganz

__________ have experienced a lot of __________ but some have still become very successful and have been able to __________ huge amounts of money for education or __________. For example, Oprah Winfrey is the __________ of many educational organisations and has raised __________ of problems in the USA and the __________ world. She feels education for everyone will be a big __________ in changing the world and helps families who have no __________ for a good education. Thus Oprah is a __________ for __________ generous African-American celebrities.

5 Synonyms

Replace the marked words with words which have the same or a very similar meaning.

1. Emmeline Pankhurst fought for **the right to vote** (➜ __________) for all adult women.
2. Many people say Plato was the most important **thinker** (➜ __________) of all time.
3. I did some **work without pay** (➜ __________) for a children's home in my town.
4. We decided to **start** (➜ __________) a campaign to teach teenagers about staying healthy.
5. There is no cure for some common illnesses, **for example** (➜ __________) a cold or the flu.
6. I had very good medical **care** (➜ __________) at the hospital.

6 Word formation

Change the words given to the form in brackets.

1. to discover ➜ (noun) __________
2. to behave ➜ (noun) __________
3. leader ➜ (verb) __________
4. to cure ➜ (noun) __________
5. recognition ➜ (verb) __________
6. award ➜ (verb) __________
7. rebel ➜ (verb) __________
8. major ➜ (noun) __________
9. to found ➜ (noun) __________
10. end ➜ (verb) __________

7 Prepositions

Fill in the right prepositions.

1. I hope that one day they will find a cure __________ HIV.
2. Your parents are nice. Why do you always rebel __________ them?
3. Many people want to be involved __________ our new project.
4. People say that he is responsible __________ his sister's death.

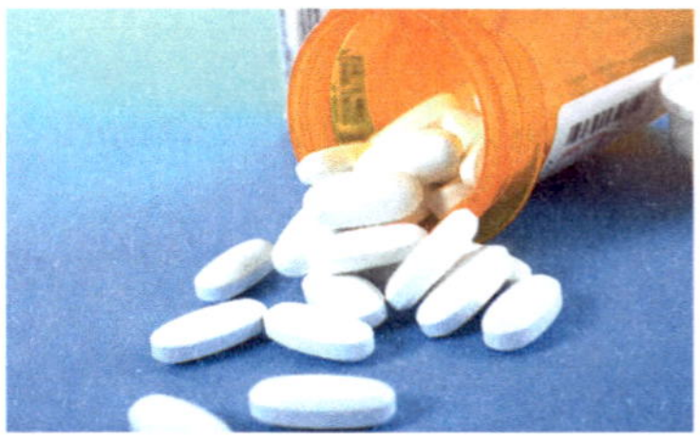

→ pages 94–95

What do you remember?

männlich • Rede • faulig • Ereignis • verbunden mit • Privatschulen (GB) • Gasse • Elite • gehören zu • ähneln • unwahrscheinlich • bombardieren • blockieren • eine Abkürzung nehmen durch • weiblich

I want to give a ______________ about different kinds of schools. Some schools are ______________ success. The ______________ send their children there. The most expensive private schools in Britain are actually called ______________ and are for ______________ or for ______________ students only. If you go to one of these, you ______________ a kind of club. It's very ______________ that you won't be successful in life. An English girl I know has a story that ______________ Josie Alibrandi's: to get to school she ______________ a forest and walked along a ______________. One day some pupils from a free school ______________ her way and ______________ her with ______________ tomatoes. She understands how they felt but it was a horrible ______________.

8 Synonyms

Replace the marked words with words which have the same or a very similar meaning.

1. We put the chairs in five long **lines** (→ ______________).
2. It is a useful quality if you can **feel** (→ ______________) tensions between people.
3. I was asked to give a speech, but I'm afraid I don't have anything **special** (→ ______________) to say.
4. **To be honest** (→ ______________), I don't think he will get good marks in the test.
5. You **look like** (→ ______________) my little brother.
6. I stopped being friends with Jamie because I didn't want to be **connected** (→ ______________) with his crimes.

9 Mixed bag: Different countries

Fill in the right words.

female • break • right to vote • dictatorship • trial • law • male

In some countries you are not allowed to voice your opinion. People have the ______________, but elections are often manipulated. If you ______________ the ______________, you can't expect a fair ______________, and ______________ citizens don't have the same rights as ______________ ones. I don't like some things about our country but I'm glad we don't live in a ______________!

→ pages 94–95

What do you remember?

überziehen • stolpern über • Lachen • flüstern • Mülleimer • Kondom • verlegen • sich schämen für • entsetzt • Lippen • antippen • Leidenschaft • vom Unterricht ausgeschlossen werden • Zeitpunkt

We all felt so ______________ the day the teacher told us how to ______________ a ______________ ! Everybody started to ______________ but the teacher said love and ______________ were nothing to ______________ and we should speak up. Then there was a really loud ______________ from the back of the class. I bit my ______________ so that I wouldn't laugh too but then someone ______________ me on the shoulder and I couldn't stop myself. I was ______________ ! I thought I would ______________ ! The teacher walked towards me but then he ______________ the ______________ and fell down. Of course, by that ______________ everyone was laughing. Poor teacher!

10 Odd word out

Which word does not fit? Cross it out and explain why.

1. to whisper • to trip over • to lean forward • to cut through

   ______________ does not fit, because ______________

2. flattered • reserved • embarrassed • ashamed

   ____

3. Prime Minister • leader of the opposition • dictatorship • voter

   ____

4. to voice one's opinion • to put no effort into sth • to rebel against • to be involved in

   ____

5. road • lane • street • row

   ____

11 Prepositions

Fill in the missing prepositions.

1. Due ________ the rainy weather, not many people went out to vote yesterday.
2. Crime is often associated ________ drugs.
3. She put no effort ________ her homework and it was very bad.
4. I don't want to be influenced ________ other people's opinions.
5. He behaved badly and was ashamed ________ his actions later.
6. Put your coat ________ . It's freezing outside!

→ pages 94–95

What do you remember?

enttäuscht • sich die Mühe machen • Partei • leidenschaftlich • die beste Partei an die Macht wählen • Wahlrecht • Wähler • sich glücklich schätzen • ungültige Stimme • ehrlich gesagt • Was ist das Problem? • Versprechen • sich anmelden • beinflusst werden von • sich leisten

Should we ________________ because we have the ________________ ? Many people don't know which ________________ they should vote for and they don't ________________ to vote or they put in a ________________ . Others don't even ________________ to become a ________________ . ________________ , I understand that point of view. I'm not ________________ about politics and I've often been ________________ by politicians. You can't believe all their ________________ and I don't want to ________________ words that are not true. However, I always vote. Some parties really are better than others and I want to ________________ . We can't ________________ to let the worst parties run our country. It only takes a few minutes to vote, so ________________ ? Just do it!

12 A crossword

Find the right words by completing the sentences below.

Across

2. The city library has … in the suburbs, too.
3. You … my brother. He has red hair, too.
7. No boys! This club is for … members only.
8. I'll never forget that … when our school won the debating competition.

Down

1. Walk down that … to get to the church.
4. It's an … school and it's extremely expensive.
5. I'm going to give a … . Please don't sleep while I'm talking!
6. They're really interested in … culture.

→ pages 94–95

What do you remember?

Premierminister/-in • Gerichtsverfahren • Diktatur • ahnungslos • vulgär • Einparteiensystem • unterhaltsam • die eigene Meinung äußern • beachten • Oppositionsführer/-in • ein Land regieren • einrichten • gegen das Gesetz verstoßen • Mitspracherecht haben • sich keine Mühe geben mit

We have some bad political parties but I'm glad we don't live in a ______________ . The people who ______________ need to know that they must ______________ of what the voters want. The ______________ has to know that there is always a ______________ ready to take over his or her job. I would hate to live in a ______________ where you can't ______________ . In our system everyone can ______________ , even if sometimes nobody listens. You don't ______________ by saying what you think and even the worst criminals get a ______________ . I think we should ______________ a Speaker's Corner in our city. I love the one in London. Well, some speakers are ______________ and ______________ their speech, or they say ______________ things, but most are clever and ______________ .

13 Say it in a different way

Use the words on the right to say the sentences in a different way.

1. She didn't work hard at all on her homework. — to put • effort

____

2. You should be glad that you live in such a nice place. — to call • lucky

____

3. He wasn't allowed to come to school for a month. — to be suspended

____

4. They live in a country which allows only one political party. — one-party system

____

5. If you want things to change, it's important to say what you think. — to voice • opinion

____

6. He really loves politics. — to be passionate

____

14 Find the missing word

1. child – childhood • adult – ______________
2. month – monthly • year – ______________
3. yesterday – tomorrow • past – ______________
4. ignorance – ignorant • passion – ______________
5. philosophy – philosopher • biology – ______________
6. party – member • state – ______________
7. to write – book • to give – ______________
8. to breathe – nose • to kiss – ______________

→ page 97

What do you remember?

Geschwister • stattfinden • Landkreis • Preisträger • Kleinkinder • von • Talentwettbewerb • Einwohner • unterstützen • Spenden • häufig • jmdn. das Leben kosten

Every year there are awards in our ________ for school groups who make a difference, and we want to be the ________ this year! We are organising a ________ which will ________ next Saturday evening. All local ________ are invited. It's free but we will ask for ________ to help a children's charity. We know that some dangerous illnesses are still ________ in some countries and ________ many people. We want to help children who have lost parents or ________ through illness. More than one ________ ten children in Africa has lost a parent and many ________ will never grow up in a family. We want to ________ the people who help them.

15 Word formation

Change the words given to the form in brackets.

1. to win → (noun) ________
2. to donate → (noun) ________
3. centre → (adjective) ________
4. to vote → (noun) ________
5. embarrassed → (adjective) ________
6. to entertain → (noun) ________
7. to ignore → (adjective) ________
8. to speak → (noun) ________
9. disappointing → (verb) ________
10. horror → (adjective) ________

16 Mixed bag: Aid awards

Complete the dialogue with words from exercise 15.

Pauline: Hey, Ken, I heard the City Improvers were the ________ of this year's Aid Awards.

Ken: Yes, we won it for our maintenance work on the old Town Hall. Some people wanted to destroy it and build a car park but we believe it's important to have historic buildings in ________ parts of the city. I think only ________ people want to destroy them. And there are too many car parks anyway.

Pauline: Well done! I totally agree with you. But you need a lot of money for your project . Where did you get it from?

Ken: We got a lot of ________ from individuals as well as big companies. We are putting on a comedy show in the Town Hall to thank people who helped. I'm sure it will be great ________!

→ page 97

What do you remember?

zentral • Instandhaltung • Helfer • aufräumen • seinem Namen alle Ehre machen • Ebene • enttäuschen • renovieren • Gott • reparieren • sich anmelden • Mühe • leisten • sich um jmdn. kümmern

My brother is in a group called The City Improvers and they really ______________ . They ______________ all kinds of tasks on a regional ______________ : they ______________ parks and ______________ broken things at children's playgrounds, for example. They are not a religious group but they also ______________ a very old church so that people could speak to ______________ in a safer building. They mostly do ______________ work on buildings but some of their ______________ also ______________ people who need help. They have a little office in a ______________ street and if you want to ______________ to become a City Improver, you can go there. If you make the ______________ and join the group, they won't ______________ you. They're really fun people to work with.

13 A puzzle

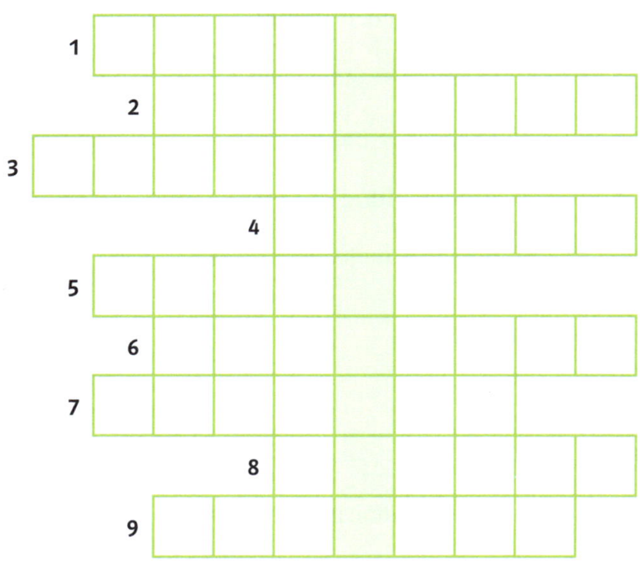

1. a kind of prize
2. to make a room or or building look more attractive
3. a brother or sister
4. a natural ability to do something well
5. an area smaller than a country but normally big enough to include some towns
6. a person who lives in a town or neighbourhood
7. to do something, e. g. a task or a service
8. a very young child
9. a very strong belief or feeling

Solution: ______________________________

→ page 100

What do you remember?

inspirierend • Aufgaben • befriedigend • Wahlkampfparole • selten • historisch • Mehrheit • charismatisch • jmdn. für sich gewinnen • Ruf • Zitate • Verantwortung • Abkürzung

Politicians give speeches all the time but they are ______ really ______. However, some politicians have a ______ for great speeches. You can call a speech ______ if people use your words in ______ years later. If you want to win an election, you also need to have a good ______. The people who have the ______ for writing these have one of the most important ______ in politics. A slogan is a kind of ______ to the opinions or values of a politician. It can help to make him or her more ______. The ______ people will always think of Barack Obama when they hear the words "yes, we can." That slogan really ______ people ______, and that must be very ______ for him and for whoever thought of it.

18 Word stress

Put the words into the right box.

prosperity • reputation • unpopular • opposition • disappointed • necessity • majority • entertaining • charismatic • appreciate

• ● • •	• • ● •

19 Mixed bag

Complete the sentences with words from exercise 18.

1. I was ______ by her speech. I had expected something better.
2. Why do politicians think we only care about ______?
   I think peace is more important than wealth.
3. He was an ______ president and he didn't win the second election.
4. The ______ of people are worried about the future.
5. People liked her speech because she was ______ but she didn't really say very much.
6. If you get a ______ for being a good speaker, you will be invited to speak everywhere.

→ page 100

What do you remember?

unpopulär • schätzen • Notwendigkeit • Senator • wohlhabend • laut, gemäß • effektiv • opfern • Ära • Es ist offensichtlich, dass … • kämpfen • Wohlstand • den Anforderungen von etw. nachkommen • gemeinsames Ziel

__________ people would prefer to be __________ than to be poor.

Vote for me if you want to protect the peace and __________ of our country. Only I can __________ of this difficult time, this special __________ in our history. We all __________ the freedom this country gives us and we have a __________ : to protect that freedom. __________ recent economic data we may have to __________, but we will never have to __________ our wonderful lifestyle.

I won't make __________ changes or tell you that war is a __________ . I was an __________ and good __________ and I'll be a great president!

20 A crossword: Political words

Across	Down
3. Suffrage is the right to …	1. What adjective describes a system where people can vote for the party they like best?
4. Giving money to a charity or a political party is called making a … .	2. What do you call a phrase that is often repeated in ads or in a political campaign?
8. If a politician wants to make his or her country totally different, he or she wants to … it.	5. If 'to elect' is the verb, what is the noun?
9. What do you call a system where people cannot vote freely because there is no opposition?	6. What do you call the ruler of an empire?
10. What do you call a political party that is not part of the current government?	7. What do politicians often make and sometimes break?

→ page 101

What do you remember?

Verfilmung • Kriterium • Titelblatt • erscheinen • originales Filmmaterial • basieren auf • Macher • Rolle • etw. mit etw. verwechseln • abhalten von • es nicht so genau nehmen mit

We are making a film ______ the life of a historical figure but you shouldn't ______ it ______ the real story of his life. We are ______ with some facts and we are not using any ______ of his public speeches, for example. This is a ______ and not a documentary. However, as the ______ of the film, we want to show the world what a great man he was. We feel the main ______ for a successful film is a great story and nothing will ______ us ______ telling this one! Top star Henry Strong plays the ______ of our hero and we expect him to ______ on the ______ of all the big film magazines very soon.

21 Prepositions

Match the sentence beginnings and endings using the right prepositions.

You are taking liberties The film is based Nothing will keep us Don't confuse fact I don't believe humans can communicate It's not easy to win people	+	on over with from	+	my life. fiction. making this film. for our film project. animals. the truth.

1. ______
2. ______
3. ______
4. ______
5. ______
6. ______

22 Mixed bag: A documentary

Complete the words.

My uncle was the m ______ of a really good documentary about the c ______ way some farm animals are treated. When it came out, it was on the c ______ of all kinds of magazines. He didn't use actors or create new film material. It was all o ______ f ______. He said almost everyone's main c ______ when they buy food is price, and he wanted to make people think about more than that.

→ page 101

What do you remember?

wildern • grausam • gründen • kommunizieren mit • Dschungel • verringern • Methoden • aussterben • handeln

Every year, many types of animals may ________________ . Most are tiny animals we have never heard of but we still need to ________________ , because we are part of the problem. If we ________________ the space wild animals have to live in, for example by cutting down huge parts of the ________________ , where should they go? Some people ________________ protected animals to make money, so never buy illegal animal products. Their ________________ for killing the animals may be very ________________ , too. It's important to ________________ other people about this, so why not get together and ________________ an action group?

23 Say it in a different way

Use the words and phrases on the right to say the sentences in a different way.

1. I hope that polar bears will never die out. **to become extinct**

____

2. We are making the amount of jungle on our planet smaller every day. **to reduce**

____

3. His ways of communicating are very strange. **methods**

____

4. I'm afraid you are not exactly telling us the truth. **to take liberties with**

____

5. Everybody accepts that businesses exist to make money. **to think it's a given**

____

6. We all want the same thing: to live in peace. **to have a common purpose**

____

24 Words and their definitions

Complete the sentences.

1. To ________________ means to hunt animals illegally.
2. A huge tropical forest is called a ________________ .
3. The opposite of 'kind' is ________________ .
4. The plural form of 'criterion' is ________________ .
5. '________________' is another word for being clean.

→ pages 102–105

What do you remember?

glücklich • Todesstrafe • inspirieren • inspirierend • gegen • Beitrag • Globalisierung • Lücken

It would be good to make a ______________ to society in some way, but how? I could fight against something I'm ______________, like ______________ for example, or I could try to help people who are poor, and not as ______________ as me. The problem is, there are too many ______________ in my knowledge. For example, is ______________ a good or a bad thing for the world's poorest people? Sometimes the people who fight against it ______________ me, but at other times I find successful business people ______________, and they love the global market! Maybe I need to work on my own understanding before I start to help others.

25 Opposites

Find the opposites of the following words.

1. often • ______________
2. paid work • ______________
3. poverty • ______________
4. past • ______________
5. male • ______________
6. childhood • ______________
7. convenient • ______________
8. to begin • ______________

26 Using proverbs

Choose one of the proverbs in the box to comment on the following situations.

Love makes the world go round. • Actions speak louder than words. • Many hands make light work. • Charity begins at home. • Do as you would be done by. • Virtue is its own reward.

1. Henry decided not to tell Jenny's secret. He wouldn't like it if someone told others his secrets.

   ____

2. Kerry never talks about social problems but she helps poor people at a centre for the homeless.

   ____

3. If we all work on this together, we will finish the job in less than an hour.

   ____

4. Nobody thanked Paul for helping the old man, but he felt good about it anyway.

   ____

5. Louise doesn't do any volunteer work but she spends every Saturday with her sick grandmother.

   ____

6. If I love you and you love me, we can achieve anything!

   ____

→ pages 102–105

What do you remember?

zurückrufen • eine Nachricht entgegennehmen • Institutionen • besetzt • Anrufbeantworter • unbequem • erfahren • Besprechung • jmdn. durchstellen • Beschwerde • Autovermietung • warten • sich nach etwas erkundigen

Some people are hard to contact by phone. Either you always get the ______ or someone tells you, "I'm sorry, she's in a ______ . Would you like her to ______ ?" What I really dislike is when they say, "I'll ______ you ______ . Please ______ ," and then you wait and wait and wait … I understand that it might be an ______ time but they shouldn't let you wait forever. Usually, if you're phoning a business, like a ______ company, and you want to ______ something, there is always someone who can talk to you or ______ , but if you're angry and you want to make a ______ , you soon ______ that nobody wants to talk to you! However, some ______ are easier to reach than some private people. When I call my friend Mary, the line is always ______ !

27 Mixed bag: Working at an animal shelter

Complete the words.

In the p ______ four or five months I have read more than one news story about animals that had e ______ from a p ______ or a zoo. For the people who work at the a ______ s ______ , caring for lost animals is part of the daily r ______ . I think that would be a good job if you only had to look after sweet animals with soft f ______ , like cats or r ______ , but there are some animals that I really don't like. A job that i ______ tasks like feeding a crocodile or a s ______ is not the right job for me! Maybe I should look for something else.

28 Prepositions

Complete the sentences with the right preposition.

1. Hello, is this the bike rental? I want to enquire ______ renting a bike for the weekend.
2. Please hang ______ a moment. I'll put you ______ to my colleague who takes care ______ that.
3. Unfortunately, she's not there at the moment. Can she ring you ______ ?
4. No, sorry, I can't wait ______ that. I'd need the bike right away.

→ pages 106–107

What do you remember?

Kritik • Ziel • Mission • gegenüberstehende Seite • Herangehensweise • analysieren

Organisations with a ______________ often need donations to pay for their activities. For this, they use ads. Their ______________ is to show people why it's a good idea to donate to them. They have to ______________ people's opinions about their mission and decide what the best type of advertising is. Should they use a shocking ______________ or a soft one? Sometimes there will be ______________ of their ads. For example, if their aims are political, there is usually an ______________, which says that what the organisation is doing is not a good thing. Marketing your mission is an interesting job!

29 Words and their definitions: How to make a difference

a) *Match the words from the box with the right definitions.*

to make a case for sth • speech • foundation • to voice one's opinion • to aid • to speak out • passionate • role model • peaceful • non-violent

1.		to say what you think
2.		having very strong feelings or emotions
3.		not using violence
4.		to support
5.		to speak out for sth
6.		a talk, especially a formal one about a particular subject
7.		to give your opinion in public
8.		a person whose behaviour, attitudes etc. people try to copy
9.		the opposite of 'violent'
10.		an organisation that gives or collects money to be used for charity or medical research, for example

b) *Write down three more words from the lexical field together with their definitions.*

____

____

____

30 All about politics

Write down 15 words that have to do with politics (words from Topic 4 and/or words that you already know).

____

____

____

Solutions

Topic 1

What do you remember?
On the one hand • rights • consent • on the other hand • age limits • Figures • age of consent • marriage • court • compulsory

1 Say it in a different way
1. sentenced to life imprisonment 2. compulsory 3. banned

2 Reacting and commenting
Individuelle S-Lösungen

What do you remember?
rough • fat • scar • sort • committed a couple of crimes • robbing • talked – into • avoid • swore • regrets • resist • All right

3 Word search: Arguing and fighting
→ bully, reckless ↓ pain, injury, scar ← violent, damage ↘ struggle, blood ↙ weapon

What do you remember?
coats • gloves • spotted • immediately • security • awkward • vulnerable • Dread • chest • flooded • single – bone • backed away • reached • dragged

4 Words to do with crime and law
law: to accuse sb of sth, legal, illegal, to break a law, to ban, age limit, independence, act, rights, compulsory, self-defense, privileges
crime: illegal, injury, theft, to break a law, to attack sb, to murder sb, assault, to rob sb, to commit a crime

5 Word formation
1. to secure 2. to weigh 3. use 4. marriage 5. to connect 6. sort 7. responsible 8. theft 9. to refer (to) 10. comprehension

What do you remember?
freak out • touch • be accused of – theft • face the consequences • struggle • container • keep up • tripped • ladder • stumbled • barely – crawl • rolled – up

6 Odd word out
1. 'Scar' does not fit because you cannot wear it.
2. 'Bone' does not fit because it has nothing to do with the law.
3. 'To drag' does not fit because it is not a synonym for 'to see'.
4. 'To skip' does not fit because it has nothing to do with losing control while moving.
5. 'To freeze' does not fit because it does not describe a movement forward.

7 Opposites
1. fat 2. marriage 3. a while 4. consent 5. legal 6. a couple of 7. rough 8. up ahead, in front of

What do you remember?
stuff • envelope • went off • blame for • denied • Secure – in case • made your point • pouring • comprehension

8 Spot the mistakes
1. swore 2. committed a crime 3. Weigh 4. face the consequences

9 Words and their definitions
a) 1. c) 2. a) 3. d) 4. b)
b) 1. meanwhile 2. while 3. a while 4. all the while

What do you remember?
use – self-defense • connect • grain • weeds • hang out • layout • accomplishment

10 Synonyms
1. sort 2. flooded 3. dread 4. pick 5. barely – stumbled 6. struggle 7. nearly

11 Bits and pieces
1. accomplishment 2. security 3. comprehension 4. compulsory

12 Find the missing word
1. single 2. chest 3. glove 4. to drag

What do you remember?
troubled • entire • edge • neglected • misunderstood • look up to

13 A crossword
Across: 3. vulnerable 5. chest 7. resist 10. barely
Down: 1. glove 2. secure 4. awkward 6. troubled 8. immediately 9. dread

What do you remember?
humour • suspense • complicated • maturity • put – on • dreads • put – off • face the truth • even though • mature

14 How does the text say it?
1. even though 2. previous 3. complicated 4. sweetheart

15 Mixed bag: First date
sweetheart • doughnut • nearly • spilled • scribbled • Say • straight – away • deal

What do you remember?
doughnuts • straight away • last • spilled – juice – wipe – up – cloth – go mad – no doubt • scribble • except • deal • Promiscuous behaviour • Say

16 Problem page
Individuelle S-Lösungen

What do you remember?
broke up – anniversary – Honestly – habits – bothered – crashed – party • gasoline • nominations • response – speech • tempted – go for • certainly • be grateful

17 Prepositions
1. of 2. into 3. of 4. up 5. for 6. up

18 Synonyms
1. figure 2. a while 3. nearly 4. entire 5. to break up 6. even though 7. except 8. to go for 9. a couple of 10. response

What do you remember?
setting a good example • broke down • attitude towards – set – priorities • priority • confirmed – valid • frowned – daft – whereas – naive • B&B (= bed and breakfast)

19 Say it in a different way
1. I'm not to blame for what happened last summer!
2. Last night a 50-year-old man was murdered with a knife.
3. The police reported the theft of 31paintings.
4. I think drinking alcohol should be banned for people under 18.
5. If you commit a crime, you have to face the consequences.
6. After having been arrested, the thief was taken to the police station straight away.
7. The victim of the assault had to be taken to hospital because of a serious injury.

20 Words and their definitions: Crime and law
a) 1. independence 2. illegal 3. age limit 4. assault 5. compulsory 6. injury 7. theft 8. right 9. self-defense 10. legal
b) Individuelle S-Lösungen

21 Characters
Individuelle S-Lösungen

Topic 2

What do you remember?
percentage • ethnic • Bangladeshi • Black Caribbean • Black African • gang • citizens • majority • neither

1 A crossword
Across: 4. citizen 7. Pakistani 8. gang
Down: 1. data 2. perception 3. majority 5. empire 6. plantation

What do you remember?
Mass • data • descended from • slave trade • plantations • Empire • Pakistanis

2 Word pairs
1. ethnic minority 2. slave trade 3. mass immigration

3 Discussing statistics
Individuelle S-Lösungen

What do you remember?
Afro-Caribbean • runs • passion • a host of • failure • rented • no one else • aimed at • mainstream • contribute • though • wage • conditions • urge

4 Word formation
1. failure 2. rent 3. service 4. abuse 5. security 6. encounter 7. presenter, presentation 8. treatment 9. recognition 10. use

5 Mixed bag: A travel agent
rent • service • failure • abuse • encounter • security

What do you remember?
post-war • harsh treatment • rents • prejudice • abuse • homesick • prosperity • past • encounters • objected to • tasks • pressed for

6 Prepositions
1. to 2. from 3. of 4. at 5. for 6. into 7. of

7 Mixed bag: Grandmother
past • homesick • passion • content • launch • no one else • contribute

What do you remember?
origin • complexity • dividing • service • sections • throughout • Caribbean • include • institutions • launch • content

8 Say it in a different way
1. Max wants to contribute to the prosperity of his town.
2. You can find Indian restaurants throughout the city.
3. Do you understand the complexity of the situation?
4. Things were not always easy for the post-war generation.
5. The building I live in is in (a) bad condition.
6. My boss always gives me the most boring tasks (to do).

9 Synonyms
1. prosperity 2. wage 3. barber 4. runs

What do you remember?
comedian • occasional • victim • based on • in charge

10 A puzzle
1. occasional 2. failure 3. slave 4. victim 5. launch 6. mainstream 7. comedian 8. prosperity
Solution: cultures

11 Mixed bag: Asian-British
prosperity • mainstream • occasional • failure

What do you remember?
confused • prevent – from • determined • evidence • gain • interpreter • service • residents • compulsory • encourage

12 Say it in a different way
1. interpreter 2. diversity 3. figure 4. speak up 5. labelled 6. indulge in

13 Words and their definitions
1. Muslim people pray 2. live in a place 3. job it is to make other people laugh 4. introduces the guests on a TV show

What do you remember?
parades • feel strongly about • printed • hammer • rest

14 Jumbled words
books, magazines and writing: edition, to print, cookery book, concise
food and cooking: rare, mushroom, deep-fried, organic, jam, sausage

15 Word class
adjectives: concise, rare, deep-fried, organic
nouns: edition, cookery book, mushroom, jam, sausage
verbs: to print

16 Opposites
1. rare 2. to feel strongly about sth 3. spicy
4. failure 5. minority 6. to gain, to win

What do you remember?
stalls • orange juice • cookery books • roast beef • Yorkshire pudding • spicy • cuisine • porridge • tomato • baked beans • butter • vinegar • rare • well-done • mineral

17 Word pairs
1. orange juice 2. well-done steak 3. roast beef
4. Yorkshire pudding 5. baked beans 6. cookery book

18 Spot the mistakes
1. rice 2. strongly 3. Youth 4. heart 5. cuisine

What do you remember?
Hindu • wedding • Buddhism • individual • identity • Islam • Christianity • factor • Judaism • temple

19 Odd word out
1. 'Hindu' does not fit because it refers to a person and not a religious group.
2. 'Sensitive' does not fit because it does not refer to food.
3. 'Butter' does not fit because it is not a vegetable.
4. 'Factor' does not fit because it does not describe a person.
5. 'Well-done' does not fit because it has nothing to do with books.

20 Mixed bag: Who eats what?
sausages • Islam • roast beef • Hindu • Christianity • spicy

21 Words and their definitions: Ethnic diversity and the fight for equality
a) 1. immigrant 2. discrimination 3. racial equality
4. integration 5. racist 6. to campaign for
7. to tolerate 8. ancestor 9. nationality
10. extremist
b) Individuelle S-Lösungen

22 An interview
Individuelle S-Lösungen

Topic 3

What do you remember?
Global warming • climate change • raise awareness • damage – pollution • added • renewable • generate – alternative

1 Word pairs
1. acid rain 2. solar power 3. climate change
4. fresh water 5. global warming 6. recycling plant 7. natural resources 8. pure air 9. pressure group 10. toxic waste 11. poisonous gas 12. carbon dioxide

2 Word formation
1. share 2. to protect 3. emission 4. poisonous
5. waste 6. to address 7. damage 8. to differ

3 Spot the mistakes
1. environmentally 2. address 3. awareness of
4. offshore

What do you remember?
Figures • third • fresh water • pure • carbon dioxide – emissions • triple • environmentally friendly • species • become extinct

4 A quiz
1. Each person throws away about four pounds of garbage.
2. Two thirds of the earth's surface is covered by water.
3. 50 to 100 species become extinct every day.
4. The population is expected to have tripled by 2100.

5 Words about the environment
positive: to campaign for, recycling plant, renewable, blackbird, solar, pressure group, windfarm, butterfly, pure, environmentally friendly, to protect, farmers' market
negative: damage, pollution, plastic, toxic, waste, emission, to become extinct, poisonous, carbon dioxide

What do you remember?
address • toxic • Poisonous – gases • Waste • plastic • canals • butterflies • blackbirds • verse • excuse • farmers' markets • appeals to

6 A puzzle
1. global warming 2. species 3. poisonous
4. carbon dioxide 5. offshore 6. share 7. solar
8. emission
Solution: windfarm

What do you remember?
International – pressure groups • campaigning • offshore – windfarms • protect • Tomorrow • recycling plant • deserve • economy • share

7 Odd word out
1. 'Resource' does not fit because it is not an environmental problem.
2. 'People power' does not fit because it does not describe a form of energy.
3. 'To recycle' does not fit because it is not a synonym of 'to make'.
4. 'Pressure group' does not fit because it refers to a group of people and not an environmental issue.
5. 'Second' does not fit because it has nothing to do with the number 'three'.

8 Words and their definitions: Verbs
1. to generate 2. to campaign 3. to protect 4. to become extinct 5. to deserve 6. to appeal to

What do you remember?
documentary • crisis • Hawaiian • marine • seabirds • chicks • desperate • toxins • ascend • food chain • packaging • throats • last

9 Words and their definitions
1. d) 2. h) 3. f) 4. g) 5. a) 6. e) 7. b) 8. c)

10 Synonyms
1. response 2. pure 3. waste, litter 4. toxic 5. emotions 6. ascend 7. whisper 8. weep

What do you remember?
scale • litter • chain • researcher • attitudes • ignorance • aware of • clear up • surrounded by – dying • come across • items • combs • brushes • lipsticks • wrappers • plugs • keyboards

11 Plan a speech
Individuelle S-Lösungen

12 Opposites
1. international 2. response 3. fresh water 4. to clear up 5. unaware 6. to whisper 7. to weep, to cry 8. to protect

What do you remember?
response • turned up • unaware of • bits • act like • pour • butcher • whispered • ban • press • descended • ran • trade

13 Word search: Animals
→ shark, eagle, blackbird ↓ seabird ↑ butterfly, turkey ← whale ↘ dolphin ↗ monkey

14 Memory test
combs, brushes, lipsticks, wrappers, plugs, DVDs, keyboards, cups, plates, knives, forks, toys, TVs, drink bottles, pens, shoes, clocks

What do you remember?
thrilled • reusable – cotton • biodegradable • litter • pollute • speaker • felt • emotion • speech • madness • rate • emotive • oxygen • Repetition • degrade

15 Word pairs
1. to be aware of 2. to appeal to 3. to be surrounded by 4. to feel strongly about 5. to be thrilled with 6. to raise awareness of 7. to clear up 8. to campaign for

16 Find the missing word
1. speech 2. emotive 3. chick 4. lipstick 5. toxic 6. to ascend

What do you remember?
college vacation • ranch • make – living • breeding • drilling • supper • ham • turkey • baked potatoes • insist • pride • spectacular – setting • meadow • stroke • blow

17 Word formation
1. insistent 2. distant 3. drive 4. to refer (to) 5. pride 6. to lease 7. characterization 8. wondrous, wonderful 9. drilling 10. creature, creation

18 Synonyms
1. career 2. extract – ranch – vacation 3. fix 4. shipped in 5. anyhow 6. ahead of

What do you remember?
puzzled • intruding • matter • letter • mineral rights • lately • lease • drilling • methane • gets trapped • underground • lease • period of time • check out • so-called • whatever

19 Say it in a different way
1. Salt water floods the land and everything dies.
2. People are of the opinion that drilling benefits the town.
3. Some of the machines have been functioning for many years.
4. When we arrived, the restaurant was deserted.
5. Sometimes it is difficult to characterize the protagonists in a story.

20 Describing landscapes and the natural world
adjectives: distant, wondrous, spectacular, heavenly, deserted
nouns: shoulder (of rock), creature, meadow, stone, ground

What do you remember?
turns off • set off • ground • are removing • amounts • stones • flood • salt • single • leak • drive • creatures • In fact • drive on

21 Prepositions
1. off 2. across 3. up 4. down 5. up 6. up

22 Odd word out
1. 'Ham' does not fit because it is not an animal but the meat from one.
2. 'Deserted' does not fit because it is rather negative.
3. 'Salt' does not fit because it is not a gas.
4. 'Layer' does not fit because it has nothing to do with the written word.

What do you remember?
deserted • deal • benefit • ship in • labor • not yet • gas drillers • run dry • functioning • fix

23 A puzzle: Verbs
1. blow 2. stroke 3. join 4. breed 5. function 6. sigh 7. insist
Solution: to benefit

24 Find the missing word
1. literature 2. front 3. puzzled 4. to blow 5. to lease 6. extract

What do you remember?
characterize • ahead • drops • front – windshield • attorneys • informal • bar owners • literature • lasting • look set

25 Words and their definitions
a) 1. supper 2. potato 3. ham 4. meadow 5. attorney 6. windshield 7. bar owner
b) Individuelle S-Lösungen

26 Opposites
1. to fix, to mend 2. to drive on 3. to lower 4. deserted 5. distant 6. to set off 7. previous 8. future 9. ahead of, in front of 10. informal

What do you remember?
Oscar-winning • rarely • writer • jury member • debate • weigh up • effective • fellow • avoid – preaching • urgent • nuclear energy • reduce • carbon

27 Word formation
1. to dramatise 2. powerful 3. humanity 4. writer 5. image, imagery 6. effective 7. urgent 8. weight

28 How does the text say it?
1. fellow 2. debate 3. are unlikely to get 4. dramatised 5. humanity 6. imagery

What do you remember?
film genres • animations • real-life • Big-budget • powerful • combined • humanity • striking – imagery • releases • dramatised • global • stocks • condemnation • overpopulation • boast

29 Word search: Film words
→ filmmaker ↓ release, (to) dramatise, big-budget ↑ real-life, message ← imagery, striking ↗ animation ↖ genre

What do you remember?
include • whenever • footprint • pork sausage • According to • dairy products • found • transportation • creates • household • result • consumption • agricultural • grow • harvest • responsible • greenhouse gas

30 Memory test
1. pasta, pork sausage, peppers, cheese, shallots 2. chicken, fish or eggs 3. vegetables

31 Noun suffixes
-ity: responsibility **-ness:** madness **-tion/-sion:** production, repetition, reduction, pollution, emission **-ment:** measurement **-ance/-ence:** influence, difference

What do you remember?
total • diet • account for • relatively • reduction • Several • studies • heated – greenhouses • growers • energy efficient • tomatoes • lettuce • production

32 Word formation
1. reduction 2. influential 3. to grow 4. to produce 5. consumption 6. to matter 7. to transport 8. specialist 9. offender 10. shortage

33 Spot the mistakes
1. tomatoes 2. relatively 3. per capita 4. replaced with

34 Units of measurement
1. slice 2. grams 3. pint 4. millilitres 5. bottle 6. kilogram

What do you remember?
Consumers • habits • ethical • electrical goods • groceries • evaluated • calculator • case • covers • slice • litres • wine • shirt • pint • beef • turn – into

35 A puzzle: Food
1. vegetables 2. pepper 3. tomato 4. pasta 5. dairy products 6. condiment 7. beef
Solution: lettuce

What do you remember?
Though • worldwide • offender • cubic metres • per capita • wheat • minimise • keen to • wastage • complicated – calculations • recycle • fertilisers

36 Words and their definitions
1. impact 2. focus 3. to replace 4. to cut 5. to remain 6. to affect 7. to be missing 8. fertilisers 9. water shortage

37 Find the missing word
1. dairy product 2. wheat 3. beef 4. chairperson 5. consumer 6. millilitre 7. slice 8. twice

What do you remember?
Units of measurement • non • kilograms • kilometres • square miles • Volume • equivalent • in existence • length

38 Odd word out
1. 'Inch' does not fit because it does not refer to volume.
2. 'By chance' does not fit because it does not describe a way of moving.
3. 'Gasoline' does not fit because it is not a gas.
4. 'To report' does not fit because it has nothing to do with counting.

39 Prepositions
1. of 2. up 3. to 4. in 5. on 6. by

What do you remember?
ounce • inches • Petrol • gallons • factors • calculate • carbon units • hypothetical • majority • option • neutral

40 Mixed bag
1. kilometre 2. square miles 3. kilograms 4. rise in temperature 5. abbreviation 6. equivalent to 7. in existence 8. volume – to flush

41 Word formation
1. cut 2. length 3. to emit 4. allergic 5. illness 6. majority 7. to consider 8. calculator, calculation

What do you remember?
in a nutshell • cruise liner • multiplying • sea change • in the ocean • all at sea • the tide • make waves • people stop and think • technology • prosperity • duty • reuse

42 Synonyms
1. to find 2. prosperity 3. option 4. minority 5. wage 6. to create 7. though 8. per capita 9. to consider 10. sore

43 Idioms
a) 1. a) 2. b) 3. c)
b) 1. in a nutshell 2. all at sea 3. a sea change

What do you remember?
elbow/wrist • wrist/elbow • thumb • sprained • ankle • heel • cuts • bruises • cheek • ache • allergy • rash • sore

44 A puzzle: At the doctor's
1. symptom 2. X-ray 3. specialist 4. blood sample 5. injection 6. homeopathic 7. ointment 8. diagnosis 9. antibiotic
Solution: treatment

What do you remember?
stung/bitten • bitten/stung • swollen • chemist's • inflamed • pills • side effects • heal up • diarrhoea • infection • blocked up • hay fever

45 Talking about your body
a) 1. wrist 2. elbow 3. cheeks 4. ankle 5. thumb
b) 1. side effects 2. to heal up 3. hay fever 4. diarrhoea 5. inflamed

46 Words and their definitions: Environmental issues
a) 1. methane 2. recycling plant 3. acid rain 4. climate 5. ozone layer 6. toxin 7. wastage 8. greenhouse gas 9. reusable 10. chemical
b) Individuelle S-Lösungen

47 A quiz
1. Friends of the Earth 2. global CO_2 emissions 3. consumer throwaway living 4. produce oil 5. salt water 6. a) litre, millilitre b) degree Celsius c) kilometre, metre, centimetre d) kilogram, gram 7. methane 8. small talk 9. antibiotics

Topic 4

What do you remember?
the majority of • oppressed • policy • racial separation • struggle • since then • widely • international • producer • diamonds • financial sector • a variety of • tourism • industry • landmarks • diverse • countryside

1 Word formation
1. descent 2. to symbolize 3. to struggle 4. diverse 5. producer 6. wealthy 7. industry 8. origin 9. natural 10. belief

2 Synonyms
1. symbolizes 2. wealthy 3. sector 4. policies 5. majority 6. descent 7. peoples

What do you remember?
Afrikaans • unlike – Dutch • Dutch – traders • townships • symbolize • South African • flag • transition of power • rethink • World Cup

3 Spot the mistakes
1. beliefs 2. stopover 3. wildlife 4. unlike

4 Prepositions
1. to 2. from 3. of 4. for 5. on

5 Bits and pieces
1. resources 2. republic 3. activist 4. countryside

What do you remember?
cycling • either – or • mines • mineral resources • republic • freedom-activist • negotiate • manufacturing • stopover point – spice route

6 Say it in a different way
1. commercial 2. brutal 3. diverse 4. exports 5. belongs 6. symbolizes 7. Tourism

What do you remember?
political • resistance • formed • ban • prohibited • attend – meetings • underground • arrests • jail sentences • trial • freedom fighters • visionary • nation-builder

7 Word pairs
1. to write an autobiography 2. to arrest a criminal 3. to be sentenced to jail 2. to contain useful information 5. to attend a meeting 6. to work as a civil servant 7. to be deprived of one's rights

8 Opposites
1. to export 2. minority 3. unlike 4. to export 5. to prohibit 6. wealthy 7. countryside 8. complicated

What do you remember?
annual – levied • booklet • at a time • policemen • unemployed • mass • walk – process • certain – persecuted • affect

9 Synonyms
1. complicated 2. prohibited 3. armed 4. fine 5. effort 6. jail

10 Words and their definitions
1. visionary 2. fine 3. to be unemployed 4. resistance 5. to persecute 6. autobiography

What do you remember?
released • documentary • celebration • former • move on • precisely – recalls • phase • excerpt • verse

11 Odd word out
1. 'Republic' does not fit because it is not a kind of job.
2. 'Industry' does not fit because it is not connected with crime and law.
3. 'To trace' does not fit because it is not a synonym for 'to treat badly'.
4. 'Trader' does not fit because it does not describe a person who wants to change something in society.
5. 'Afrikaans' does not fit because it is a language and not a country.

12 Word families
1. release – to release 2. accompaniment – to accompany 3. statement – to state 4. celebration – to celebrate 5. fight, fighter – to fight 6. resistance – to resist

What do you remember?
destinations • game reserve • ranks with • diversity • species • ensures • safaris • includes • magnificent • scenic • vegetation • accommodation • varying from • stay • traditional • staff • comfort

13 A puzzle: Words to do with wildlife
1. snake 2. mammal 3. species 4. elephant 5. safari 6. zebra 7. reptile 8. giraffe 9. lion
Solution: amphibian

What do you remember?
indigenous • archaeological site • majestic • civilization – guided • exaggerated – nearly

14 Find the missing word
1. reptile 2. Dutch 3. cycling 4. documentary 5. civil servant 6. producer

15 Noun suffixes
-ment: enjoyment, improvement **-ion:** civilization, selection **-ing:** meeting, painting **-ity:** diversity, majority **-ary:** documentary, visionary

16 Choose the right word
1. fence 2. unspoilt 3. depart 4. established 5. improvement

What do you remember?
impressive – nature reserve • established • protect • preserved • enjoyment • unspoilt • open savannah • selection • paintings

17 Odd word out
1. 'Zebra' does not fit because it does not refer to a group of different animals.
2. 'Brutal' does not fit because it is not a word that describes something positively.
3. 'Painting' does not fit because it does not have anything to do with books or the printed word.
4. 'Species' does not fit because it does not mean 'different things'.
5. 'To establish' does not fit because it does not mean to protect someone or something.

18 Which word does not fit?
1. complicated 2. wealthy 3. republic 4. contained 5. persecute

What do you remember?
HIV • healthcare • encouraging • cure • limited • likely • reduced • declining • killing • demand • ivory • educated • conservation • key • conservationists

19 A crossword
Across: 3. plumber 6. encourage 7. likely 8. carpenter
Down: 1. cure 2. reduce 4. equality 5. decline

What do you remember?
cosy • B&B • run by • advertisement • description • twin room • en-suite • lounge • equipped • require • chef • braai

20 Word search
→ en-suite, confirm ↓ double, star ↑ deposit
← reception, booking ↗ twin, single ↖ lounge

21 Prepositions
1. over 2. off 3. by 4. up 5. off 6. on

What do you remember?
star – valley • double – single • WLAN • reception • laundry • deposit – bookings • hairdryer • tourist guides • cottages • Rand

22 Say it in a different way
1. Barry ran the kitchen in a big financial institution. He then went on to become head of his own restaurant.
2. If it was up to me, I would establish an organisation to educate young people the importance of conservation from an early age.
3. The vegetation in the Cape is similar to that of the Mediterranean.
4. To secure your booking, please pay a deposit.

23 Words and their definitions
1. valley 2. vegetation 3. trader 4. conservationist 5. amphibian 6. wealthy 7. zebra 8. unspoilt 9. savannah 10. mine

24 Choose the right word
1. landscapes 2. safari 3. vegetation 4. conservationist 5. natural resource 6. mineral

Topic 5

What do you remember?
Civil disobedience • refuse • rebel against • recognize • tactic • be guilty of • citizen • philosophers • behaviour • tax • social critic • are involved in • attack • goal • non-violent

1 Odd word out
1. 'Behaviour' does not fit because it is not a person.
2. 'Tactic' does not fit because it is not an adjective.
3. 'Citizen' does not fit because it has nothing to do with being ill.
4. 'Major' does not fit because it is not an adjective of time.

2 Words and their definitions
1. criticizes aspects of society 2. you want to achieve in the future 3. environment 4. talks about a religious subject in a public place 5. studies plants and animals

What do you remember?
adulthood • such as • death sentence • antibiotic • Ever since • discovery • penicillin • treatment • International • biologists – launch • cure for • Major

3 Words and their definitions
1. to donate 2. to assassinate 3. annual 4. current 5. non-violent 6. foundation

4 Mixed bag
1. Non-violent 2. current 3. foundation 4. donate 5. annual 6. assassinate

What do you remember?
African-Americans • discrimination • donate • healthcare • founder • awareness • entire • factor • budget • trailblazer • future

5 Synonyms
1. suffrage 2. philosopher 3. volunteer work
4. launch 5. such as 6. treatment

6 Word formation
1. discovery 2. behaviour 3. to lead 4. cure
5. to recognize 6. to award 7. to rebel 8. majority
9. foundation, founder 10. to end

7 Prepositions
1. for 2. against 3. in 4. for

What do you remember?
speech • associated with • elite • public schools • male • female • belong to • unlikely • resembles • cut through • lane • blocked • bombarded • rotten • occasion

8 Synonyms
1. rows 2. sense 3. particular 4. Frankly
5. resemble 6. associated

9 Mixed bag: Different countries
right to vote • break – law • trial • female • male • dictatorship

What do you remember?
embarrassed • put on • condom • whisper • passion • to be ashamed of • laugh • lips • tapped • horrified • be suspended • tripped over • rubbish can • stage

10 Odd word out
1. 'To whisper' does not fit, because it does not describe a movement.
2. 'Reserved' does not fit because it does not describe a feeling.
3. 'Dictatorship' does not fit because it is not a person.
4. 'To put no effort into sth' does not fit because it is the opposite of taking action.
5. 'Row' does not fit because it is not a kind of street.

11 Prepositions
1. to 2. with 3. into 4. by 5. of 6. on

What do you remember?
call ourselves lucky • vote • party • bother • dummy vote • register • voter • Frankly • passionate • disappointed • promises • get influenced by • get the best party in • afford • what's the big deal

12 A crossword
Across: 2. branches 3. resemble 7. female 8. occasion
Down: 1. lane 4. elite 5. speech 6. Jewish

What do you remember?
one-party system • run a country • take notice • Prime Minister • leader of the opposition • dictatorship • voice your opinion • have a say • break the law • trial • establish • ignorant • put no effort into • vulgar • entertaining

13 Say it in a different way
1. She didn't put any effort into her homework at all.
2. You should call yourself lucky to live in such a nice place.
3. He was suspended from school for a month
4. They live in a country with a one-party system.
5. If you want things to chance, it's important to voice your opinion.
6. He is really passionate about politics.

14 Find the missing word
1. adulthood 2. yearly, annual 3. future
4. passionate 5. biologist 6. citizen 7. speech
8. lips

15 Word formation
1. winner 2. donation 3. central 4. vote, voter
5. embarrassing 6. entertainment 7. ignorant
8. speech 9. to disappoint 10. horrified, horrible

What do you remember?
county • award-winners • talent show • take place • residents • donations • frequent • take the lives of • siblings • out of • infants • aid

16 Mixed bag: Aid awards
winners • central • ignorant • donations • entertainment

17 A puzzle
1. award 2. decorate 3. sibling 4. talent
5. county 6. resident 7. perform 8. infant
9. passion
Solution: donations

What do you remember?
live up to their name • perform • level • clean up • repair • fixed up • God • maintenance • helpers • take care of • central • sign on • effort • disappoint

What do you remember?
rarely • inspiring • reputation • historic • quotes • campaign slogan • responsibility • tasks • shortcut • charismatic • majority of • won – over • satisfying

18 Word stress
• ● • • prosperity, unpopular, necessity, majority, appreciate
• • ● • reputation, opposition, disappointed, entertaining, charismatic

19 Mixed bag
1. disappointed 2. prosperity 3. unpopular
4. majority 5. charismatic 6. reputation

What do you remember?
It's a given that • prosperous • prosperity • meet the demands • era • appreciate • common purpose • According to • struggle • sacrifice • unpopular • necessity • effective • senator

20 A crossword: Political words
Across: 3. vote 4. donation 8. remake 9. dictatorship 10. opposition
Down: 1. democratic 2. slogan 5. election 6. emperor 7. promises

What do you remember?
based on • confuse – with • taking liberties • original footage • film adaptation • makers • criterion • keep – from • part • appear • cover

21 Prepositions
1. You are taking liberties with the truth. 2. The film is based on my life. 3. Nothing will keep us from making this film. 4. Don't confuse fact with fiction. 5. I don't believe humans can communicate with animals. 6. It's not easy to win people over for our film project.

22 Mixed bag: A documentary
maker • cruel • covers • original • footage • criterion

What do you remember?
become extinct • take action • reduce • jungle • poach • methods • cruel • communicate with • set up

23 Say it in a different way
1. I hope that polar bears will never become extinct.
2. We are reducing the amount of jungle on our planet every day.
3. His methods of communicating are very strange.
4. I'm afraid you are taking liberties with the truth.
5. Everybody thinks it's a given that businesses exist to make money.
6. We all have a common purpose: to live in peace.

24 Words and their definitions
1. poach 2. jungle 3. cruel 4. criteria 5. pure

What do you remember?
contribution • opposed to • capital punishment • fortunate • gaps • globalization • inspire • inspirational

25 Opposites
1. rarely 2. volunteer work 3. prosperity
4. previous 5. female 6. adulthood
7. inconvenient 8. to end

26 Using proverbs
1. Do as you would be done by. 2. Actions speak louder than words. 3. Many hands make light work. 4. Virtue is its own reward. 5. Charity begins at home. 6. Love makes the world go round.

What do you remember?
answering machine • meeting • ring back • put – through • hang on • inconvenient • car rental • enquire about • take a message • complaint • learn • institutions • engaged

27 Mixed bag: Working at an animal shelter
past • escaped • pet shop • animal – shelter • routine • fur • rabbits • includes • snake

28 Prepositions
1. about 2. on – through – of 3. back 4. for

What do you remember?
mission • aim • analyze • approach • criticism • opposing side

29 Words and their definitions: How to make a difference
a) 1. to voice one's opinion 2. passionate 3. non-violent 4. to aid 5. to make a case for sth 6. speech 7. to speak out 8. role model 9. peaceful 10. foundation
b) Individuelle S-Lösungen

30 All about politics
Individuelle S-Lösungen